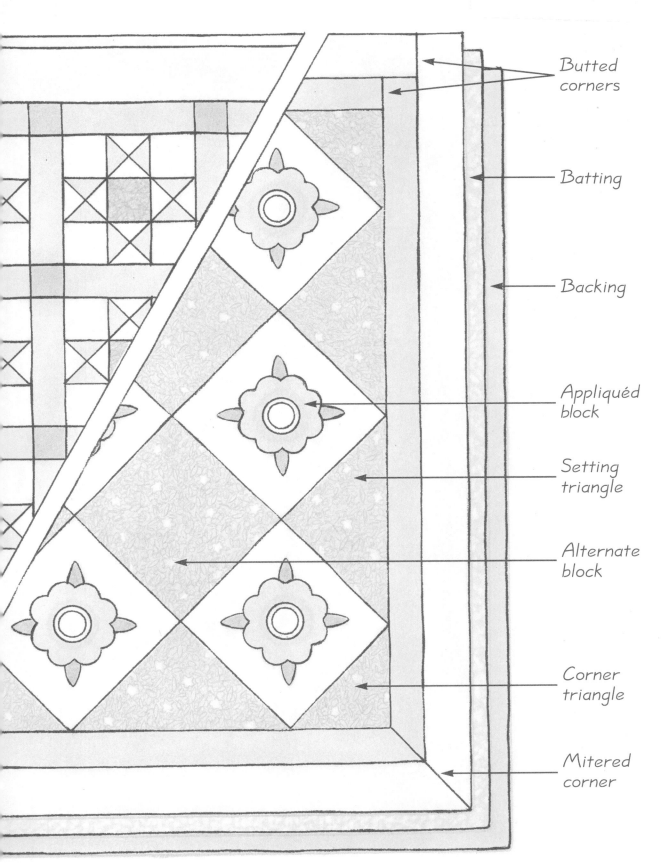

Butted
corners

Batting

Backing

Appliquéd
block

Setting
triangle

Alternate
block

Corner
triangle

Mitered
corner

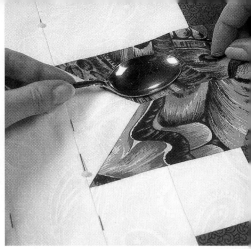
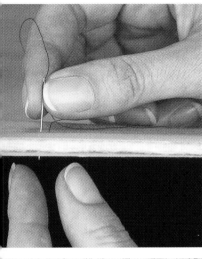

Rodale's Successful
Quilting Library®

Flawless
Hand
Quilting

Rodale Quilt
Book Editors

Rodale Press, Inc.
Emmaus, Pennsylvania

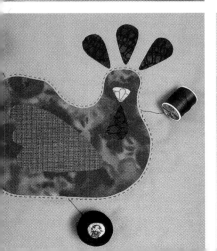
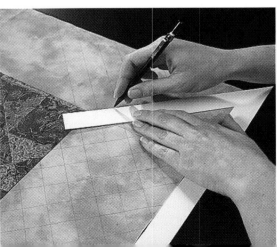

© 1999 by Rodale Press, Inc.

Printed in the United States of America on
acid-free ∞ , recycled ♺ paper

Editors: Suzanne Nelson, Ellen Pahl, Sally
    Schneider, Karen Costello Soltys, and
    Jane Townswick
Writers: Jane Hall, Dixie Haywood, Cyndi
    Hershey, Carol Johnson, Sue Linker, Gwen
    Marston, Mary Stori, Debra Wagner, Janet
    Wickell, and Darra Duffy Williamson
Interior Book Designers: Sandy Freeman and
    Sue Gettlin
Layout Designer: Keith Biery
Interior Illustrator: Sandy Freeman
Interior Photographers: John Hamel and
    Mitch Mandel
Interior Photo Stylist: Stan Green
Cover Photographer: John Hamel
Cover Designer: Sandy Freeman
Photography Editor: James Gallucci
Model: Anne Cassar
Copy Editor: Ann Snyder
Manufacturing Coordinator: Patrick Smith
Indexer: Nan Badgett
Editorial Assistance: Karen Earl-Braymer

On the cover: Spring Green by Mary Stori,
    Prospect Heights, Illinois

Rodale Home and Garden Books
Vice President and Editorial Director:
    Margaret J. Lydic
Managing Editor, Quilt Books:
    Suzanne Nelson
Director of Design and Production:
    Michael Ward
Associate Art Director: Carol Angstadt
Production Manager: Robert V. Anderson Jr.
Studio Manager: Leslie M. Keefe
Copy Director: Dolores Plikaitis
Manufacturing Manager: Mark Krahforst
Office Manager: Karen Earl-Braymer

We're always happy to hear from you.

For questions or comments concerning
the editorial content of this book, please
write to:

Rodale Press, Inc.
Book Readers' Service
33 East Minor Street
Emmaus, PA 18098

Look for other Rodale books wherever
books are sold. Or call us at (800)
848–4735.

For more information about Rodale Press
and the books and magazines we publish,
visit our World Wide Web site at:

http://www.rodalepress.com

**Library of Congress Cataloging-in-Publication
Data published the first volume of this series as:**

Rodale's successful quilting library.
    p.   cm.
Includes index.
    ISBN 0–87596–760–4 (hc: v. 1:alk paper)
    1. Quilting. 2. Patchwork. I. Soltys, Karen
Costello. II. Rodale Press.
TT835.R622 1997
746.46'041—dc21   96–51316

Flawless Hand Quilting:
    ISBN 0–87596–820–1

**Distributed in the book trade
by St. Martin's Press**

4 6 8 10 9 7 5 3   hardcover

On this page: Autumn by the Pond
by Eloise G. Smyrl, Media, Pennsylvania

Contents

Introduction

From left, Rodale Quilt Book Editors who worked on the book are Sally Schneider, Ellen Pahl, Suzanne Nelson (standing), Jane Townswick, and Karen Soltys.

The quilting frame has been the hub of social activity for women for several centuries. The simple action of moving the needle up and down through layers of fabric has been the soothing accompaniment to shared tears and triumphs, joys and sorrows. Even as the world has grown increasingly complex and more dependent on technology, and we've all grown more pressed for time, the gentle art of quilting by hand has continued to flourish.

The group you see gathered around this particular quilting frame are the Rodale Quilt Book Editors who worked together to bring you this book—*Flawless Hand Quilting*. Although over the course of a workday we spend more time in front of a computer than we do at a quilting frame, we are all avid quiltmakers who love the soothing rhythm of hand quilting. We take layered and basted quilts with us on road trips to quilt shows in Paducah, Houston, and other places in between. We have been spotted quilting at our kids' sporting events. We quilt while waiting for them at concert rehearsals. We even manage to quilt while running interference with feisty cats who think that swiping at the needle and thread is a game. We do that magical trick of quilting while watching a video, which means knowing when to look up to catch the good parts and just listening to the rest.

Our lunchtime conversations center around the best kinds of needles (the ones that don't bend and are easy to thread). We ponder the merits of different battings. We wish for a quilt fairy who could come in under cover of darkness and baste together a bed-size quilt, sparing us the backaches. We mutter about thimbles that get sweaty and go flying across the room. We count our stitches and wonder how those fabled Amish quilters manage to get 20 per inch. We admire hand stippling and trapunto and hope someday to make a quilt that is stipple quilted to within an inch of its life (it could happen!).

In short—we are typical quilters who love hand quilting.

Our goal in putting together this book was to provide the very best information on every aspect of hand quilting in one handy place. We wanted this to be a book that a quilter could grow with. If you're new to hand quilting, you'll find all the basics you need to get started. If you've gotten a little experience under your belt (or make that your thimble), we provide the next level of detail that can help you improve your technique. And if you're a master quilter, we've tried to include enough tips and tricks and new twists on old techniques so that you'll find something you've never seen before.

Because we think it's so important to *show* as well as to describe how to do a technique, we spent hundreds of hours working with writers, sample makers, and photographers to make sure that the text and the 250 photographs are as clear and accurate as they can be. Our photo stylist, Stan Green, invented a clever contraption

that allows us to show hand position from both the top and bottom of the quilt at the same time (check out pages 82 to 86). We collected quilts from some of the very best hand quilters in the country to use in the photographs that start each chapter. We hope you enjoy this inspiring show-and-tell of outstanding quilts. Whenever we received a shipment of quilts in the office, all work stopped as we gathered around to marvel at the exquisite stitching.

While all of these features are great, we think the best gift we give to you in this book is the chapter called " 'Quilt as Desired' Finally Explained." As quilters, we were tired of running into this phrase time and again and not knowing what it is we desired! After you get done reading those pages, you'll be able to look at your quilt top and easily figure out what sort of quilting you want to add.

As we worked on this book, there was a lot of talk in the news about the new millennium and the sorts of changes that would await us as we entered the brave new world of the year 2000 and beyond. There are undoubtedly big changes and exciting times ahead. In the midst of all that, it is reassuring to know that this simple stitchery travels with us as we move forward, where it will continue to bring us comfort and joy.

Suzanne Nelson

Suzanne Nelson
Managing Editor, Rodale Quilt Books

INTRODUCTION

1 The best choice for quilt backs is 100 percent cotton with a weave that is easy to quilt through. Avoid sheets since they are typically woven so tight you'll struggle to get a needle through. Busy prints camouflage stitches, a plus when you're a beginner but a hindrance when you want the quilting design to show on the back.

2 Artfully pieced backings, with blocks and bits of fabrics stitched together, create a decorative look. But when you're planning to hand quilt, think twice about what it means to stitch through all those extra seams.

3 When piecing the backing of a quilt, avoid using a center seam. When a quilt is folded in half, the extra bulk of the center seam along the fold line stresses the quilt, causing the quilt top and batting to break down even more quickly in that area. Instead, cut one of the lengths of backing fabric into two long, narrow pieces. Stitch a narrow piece to each side of the full-width piece.

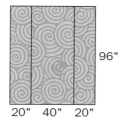

20" 40" 20"
96"

4 You don't always need to piece backings with lengthwise seams. If your quilt is 74 inches long or less, it might be more economical to piece the backing crosswise. Measure the width of the quilt, add 6 to 8 inches, then purchase two pieces of fabric that length. Cut one piece in half lengthwise and stitch each half to a long edge of the other piece.

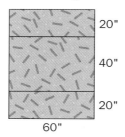

20"
40"
20"
60"

5 Quilts larger than 74 inches in both directions require three lengths of fabric for the backing, but often only a small portion of the third length is used. To save yardage, you can piece one of the three lengths. Cut two lengths full size; cut the third length half the required size. Cut this short piece in half lengthwise and sew the two resulting pieces together end to end. Piece the backing so the seams look like the letter H.

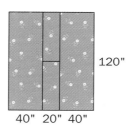

40" 20" 40"
120"

6 For seamless quilt backs, look for extra-wide quilt backing fabrics. They are available from 90 to 104 inches wide in an assortment of colors and prints.

7 Sometimes puckers and wrinkles appear around the seam in the backing fabric. To help prevent them, make sure you trim away the selvages before stitching the sections together. Sew the seam with a longer stitch than you normally use (try 10 stitches to the inch, rather than the normal 12), and press the seam open.

8 Hold a "Sizing Up the Markers" program at your quilt guild. Divide the guild into groups of 10 people. Make each person in the group responsible for finding and bringing one kind of marker and a fat quarter of muslin to the next meeting. (Assign each person a different marker.) Mark the muslin with each marker; be sure to write the name of each marker in permanent ink. Layer the muslin with batting and backing, and quilt over the lines. Wash the muslin to see how each marker reacts.

9 Maintain the point of a pencil by holding it to the fabric horizontally so it wears more on the side than on the tip. If you roll the pencil around in your hand as you

mark a line, you'll keep it sharp on all sides, meaning fewer trips to the sharpener.

10 When you start a quilting session, thread a full pack of needles onto the spool while your eyes are fresh. You can cut the length of thread you need as each needle advances to the front of the line.

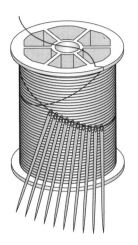

11 To avoid stopping and starting unnecessarily, set aside a needle left with a shorter thread after tying off. Use a new prethreaded needle for starting longer lines. Save the needle with the shorter thread for quilting shorter lines or places where you need to start and stop frequently.

12 Remove the quilt from the hoop or frame at the end of each quilting session to ease the tension on the fabric. If you leave it in the hoop, the section that is in the hoop can stretch, resulting in a quilt that will not lie flat.

13 Make your own protection for the hardworking finger underneath the quilt by indenting the top of an inexpensive metal thimble with a

hammer. The raised edge will help push the needle upward.

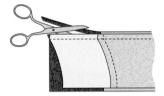

14 If possible, remove markings at the end of each quilting session even if you intend to wash the quilt when it is completed. The less time the marks have to bond with the fabric and quilting thread, the better. This is especially true with tapes used to mark the quilt. If they are left on too long, they can leave a sticky residue that is extremely difficult to remove.

15 When you plan your quilting designs, make sure some lines go right up to the binding. This simple trick will help your quilt hang better.

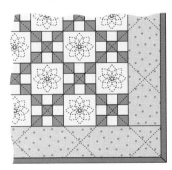

16 Trim all hanging threads from the back of the quilt top before you baste it. If you don't, dark threads can show through the lighter fabrics in the quilt top and look like dirty marks on the finished quilt. Once you have basted the quilt, there is no way to remove them—short of undoing the basting.

17 Check for shadowing in the seam allowances. Place the quilt top on a light-colored surface. Check along the seams to be sure that the seam allowance of a darker fabric doesn't shadow through the background. If it does, trim the darker fabric so that it is narrower than its opposing seam allowance.

18 Batting thickness may affect your choice of needle. For example, it may be too hard to get a very short needle through a loftier-than-normal batt, while using a long needle on a thin batt may result in longer stitches.

19 Don't try to quilt too far away from your body. Move the quilt when you start to stretch out of alignment. You'll make better stitches and be kind to your back and arm muscles. If you are quilting in a frame, move your chair or roll the quilt.

20 If you have trouble threading a needle, lick the eye of the needle instead of moistening the thread. The moisture tends to make the end of the thread swell, and if you are already having trouble threading the needle, that will make it even harder! You can also try cutting the thread at a diagonal. Sometimes the little point that results goes through the needle more easily.

Tools
of the Trade

T radition meets the twenty-first century in the process of hand quilting, which combines the best of these two diverse worlds. While the basic requirements are simple and few—a needle, thread, thimble, and scissors—modern technology adds a wealth of useful time- and labor-saving goodies to enhance the hand-stitching experience. Experiment until you find the tools and brands you like best, then treat yourself to the best quality you can afford.

Getting Ready

A key requirement for successful hand quilting is a comfortable, quilter-friendly stitching environment. Choose a well-lit, well-ventilated area. Natural light is best, but not always an option, especially if you customarily stitch at night. Supplement overhead lighting with task lighting that can be focused directly on your work.

Whether working in a frame, in a hoop, or in your lap, select a chair of comfortable height with adequate back support and with arms that do not confine or impede you. A small chairside table is ideal for corralling essential tools, while a VCR, CD, or tape player can keep you current on videos and music.

Finally: Do remember that quilting is a sedentary activity. Take an occasional break to rest your eyes, stretch, and enjoy a soothing cup of tea.

What You'll Need

Quilting needles (called betweens)

Milliner's needles (for tying)

Cotton or cotton-wrapped polyester quilting thread

Cake of beeswax

Rayon or metallic quilting thread (optional)

Quilting stencils or patterns

Ott-Lite or other task light

Thread snips or embroidery scissors

Quilt hoop or frame

Thimble

Needles

For small, consistent stitches, use special needles called betweens for hand quilting. Betweens are smaller than the average needle, with a short shaft and rounded eye. **They range in size from size 5 to 12 and come in single-size or variety packs.** The higher the number, the smaller and finer the needle. Some are easier to thread than others, so experiment with different sizes and brands until you find the one that suits you best.

Tied quilts usually involve thicker threads and heavier batting. **Try a milliner's needle, which is long and fine and has a much larger eye than a traditional sewing or quilting needle.**

Milliners

Tip

If you are a beginner, try a size 8 or 9 needle, then move on to a smaller, finer needle as your confidence and skills increase.

TOOLS OF THE TRADE

11

Cotton Thread

The best choice for hand quilting is 100 percent cotton or cotton-wrapped polyester quilting thread. Both are readily available and come in a rainbow of colors. Some brands are finished with a special coating that makes them less likely to tangle and fray and easier to thread. Look for the words "quilting thread" on the spool end.

Choose a thread color that is a little darker or a little lighter than the fabric to give the quilting more definition.

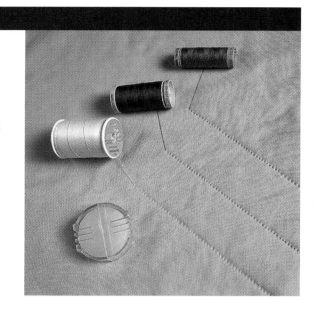

Specialty Threads

While more commonly associated with machine quilting, rayon and metallic threads adapt nicely to hand quilting. These beautiful threads create unusual textures and dazzling effects such as rain, frost, or light on water.

Specialty thread can fray easily, particularly at the eye of the needle, and the constant friction of stitching through multiple layers increases its tendency to shred. Work with a shorter-than-usual length of thread, occasionally shift the eye of the needle, and resist the urge to undo stitches!

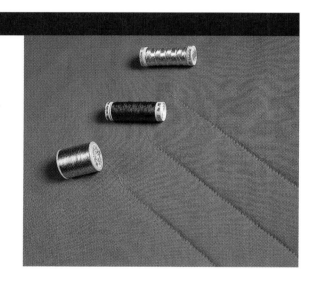

Quilting Designs

Entire publications focus on quilting motifs, and many quilt magazines include special or seasonal designs.

Perforated plastic stencils allow you to mark along the slots for elaborate feathers and wreaths—ideal for filler blocks. Border designs often include companion stencils to cope with tricky corner turns. **A close cousin of the stencil, a quilting template is a shape cut from paper, cardboard, or plastic, then traced onto the quilt top.** Simple motifs can be adapted from fabric motifs or even from coloring books or cookie cutters.

Lighting

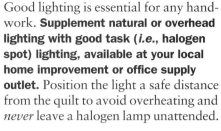

Good lighting is essential for any hand-work. **Supplement natural or overhead lighting with good task (*i.e.*, halogen spot) lighting, available at your local home improvement or office supply outlet.** Position the light a safe distance from the quilt to avoid overheating and *never* leave a halogen lamp unattended.

Increasingly popular among quiltmakers is the **Ott-Lite, a small flip-up lamp that closely simulates natural light.** In addition, it is glare- and heat-free, portable, and energy efficient.

Effort Savers

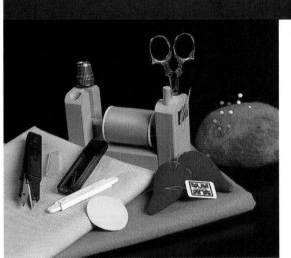

A **spool caddy** has a spindle for thread and a magnetized holder for a small scissors, thimble, and extra needles.

A **needle threader** is perfect for tiny size 12s, and a round rubber disc called a **Needle Grabber** helps to grip and pull a stubborn needle through bulky layers.

Use a **strawberry emery** to sharpen needles and a good **pincushion or case** to keep them rust-free and safe from family and pets! **Thread snips**—small, handled clippers, usually with a case—make an ideal alternative to scissors for clipping and trimming threads.

Do you always lose your thimble at meetings and bees? A round-the-neck chatelaine can help keep basic quilting notions close at hand.

Helpful Extras

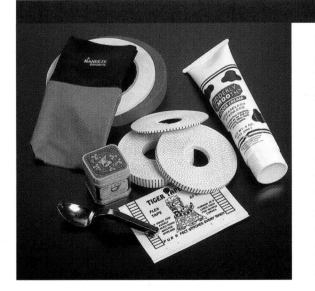

Masking tape is terrific for marking grids and straight lines. It comes in a variety of widths, including ¼ inch, just right for outline quilting. **Tiger Tape** is marked with guidelines for perfectly spaced stitches.

Use a **quilt spoon** under the quilt to create a ridge, which helps form tiny, even stitches. It also protects the underneath fingers from painful pricks.

Soothe punctured fingers with a **lanolin ointment** such as Bag Balm or Udderly Smooth Udder Cream. Finally, quilt longer and more comfortably with **therapeutic gloves** such as Handeze.

Check your local paint store for the freshest masking tape. The fresher the tape, the less likely it is to leave tape residue on your quilt.

TOOLS OF THE TRADE

I t can be hard getting used to wearing a thimble, especially if you've never stitched with one. But it's well worth the effort. A good-fitting thimble gives you more control, which translates into finer stitching. Plus, you avoid the discomfort of a sore finger. Choosing a thimble is a lot like choosing shoes—good fit and comfort are essential, and the style needs to match how you plan to use it. With all of the choices available, there's a thimble out there that will suit you to a tee.

Getting Ready

A thimble is a quilter's most personal tool. When you go shopping for a thimble, take along a small quilt sandwich to do some test quilting. Two pieces of muslin with batting in the middle are fine, or do some simple piecing to see how the thimble works when quilting through seams. Take your time and try several different kinds. Notice whether you are more comfortable pushing with the tip or side of your finger; different thimbles are suited to different motions. Spend as much time doing this test stitching as you can to make sure that the thimble will be comfortable to wear for an extended period. A thimble that stays in your sewing basket is no protection for your finger.

Gallery of Thimbles

Metal

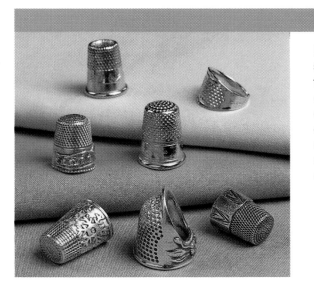

Metal, whether it is brass, stainless steel, silver, or even gold, is the traditional material for thimbles. Metal offers the best protection from the end of the needle, but a metal thimble can cause your finger to perspire. To avoid this problem or to accommodate long fingernails, try either an open-ended or ring-type design.

Stop quilting about every half hour and remove your thimble to let your finger breathe. Flex your wrists, too, to keep them limber.

Leather

Leather thimbles are a good option if you've never worn a thimble before or if you find wearing a heavier metal thimble uncomfortable. Leather thimbles are generally designed for pushing the needle with the ball of the finger. With repeat use, plain leather can wear thin, allowing the needle to poke through. For extra protection, look for ones made of goat leather or those fitted with a small metal plate inside.

Ridged Top

A thimble with a ridge around the top will hold the needle in place while you position it in the fabric and make your stitches. Because the needle does not slip, you will find it faster and easier to make even stitches. This is especially useful when rocking several stitches onto the needle at a time. Ridged thimbles are available in both leather and metal models.

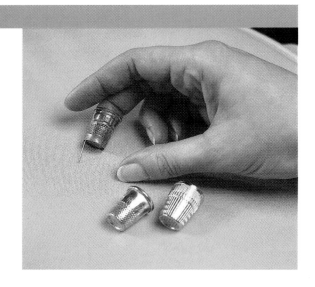

Indentations

Another way to support the needle is with the indentations, or dimples, in the top and around the sides of the thimble. Deeper indentations are more slip-proof than shallow ones. They are found in a variety of thimbles, used alone or combined with ridges. If you prefer to push with the end of your finger, find a thimble with deep dimples on the top. If you are a "side pusher," the deeper dimples should be all around the sides.

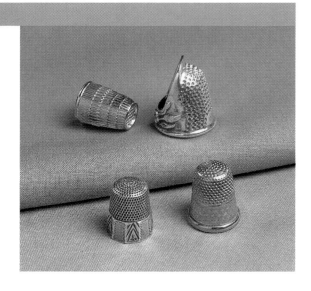

Porcelain

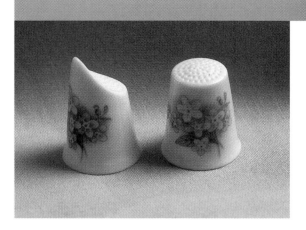

Porcelain thimbles are not just for collectors; two that are made for quilting are practical as well as attractive. With no glazing on the inside, they are cool and comfortable to wear. **Both types of porcelain thimbles have dimples with which to position the needle; the angled one is made for those who have longer fingernails.**

Tip

Porcelain thimbles are sturdy and durable, but they can break if dropped on a hard floor.

Paddle

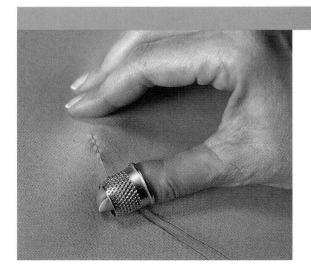

The paddle thimble is surprisingly easy to learn to use. If you have finger or wrist problems, it may be a more comfortable way to quilt.

Hold the paddle between your curved fingers and your thumb; the thumb should be in front of the stitches. Support the needle in the indentations. Take stitches with just a small back-and-forth movement of your fingers on the paddle. **You will need to set the first stitch with your fingers before you quilt with the paddle thimble.**

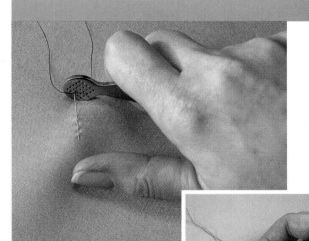

Tip

With a little practice, you can use the paddle to quilt away from your body, making it well suited to quilting in a floor frame.

Open Top

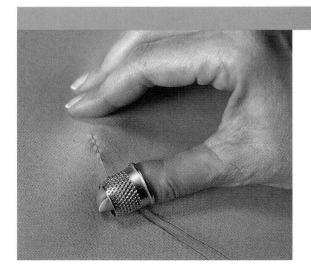

This open-top thimble, also known as a tailor's thimble, is meant to be worn on your thumb, allowing you to quilt in any direction. With practice you can learn to quilt away from yourself, from left to right (if you are right-handed), or right to left (if you are left-handed), as well as in the naturally more comfortable directions.

CHOOSING THE RIGHT THIMBLE

17

Protecting the Finger Underneath

For totally pain-free quilting, there are ways to protect the finger underneath the quilt from pokes and pricks. **Finger wraps or adhesive-backed metal or plastic shields protect the finger, while allowing you to feel the needle pressure.** Metal, porcelain, or plastic protectors are also designed to push the needle upward as it hits an angled top. This type not only protects the finger but also helps form the stitch. If at first these protectors don't feel totally comfortable, stick with them. It takes some practice to get the feel for using them.

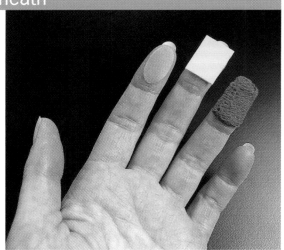

Tips for the Thimble Impaired

Getting a Good Fit

Tip

When you are trying on thimbles, give your hand a gentle shake. The thimble should not fall off. If it does, it's too loose.

A thimble should be snug enough to stay on your finger as you work but not so tight it's uncomfortable. **The perfect-fitting thimble is one that just touches the end of your nail without crowding your finger and will not fall off when you tip your finger downward.** Inexpensive metal thimbles usually come in just Small, Medium, and Large sizes, while more expensive ones and porcelain thimbles offer a wider size variety. Many leather thimbles come in one-size-fits-all and will conform to the shape of your finger.

Learning to Use a Thimble

It is not only painful, it is almost impossible to form even stitches without using a thimble. **Start the learning process by putting inexpensive metal or plastic thimbles on all four fingers of your quilting hand, then quilt on a practice piece.** With one on each finger, you can't cheat and quilt with a finger that doesn't have a thimble! Once you become used to pushing with a thimble, graduate to using a thimble on just one finger. If it still seems unnatural, wear the thimble all day, regardless of your activities, until you no longer are aware of it on your finger.

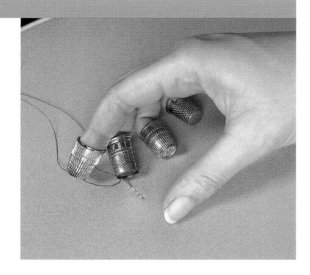

The Quilter's
Problem Solver

When Good Thimbles Go Bad

Problem	Solution
Holes eventually wear in metal and leather thimbles.	This is a sign that you have a consistent quilt stitch (congratulations!) and that you've spent a lot of time on your quilting (again, a reason to rejoice). Any material subject to repeated pressure in the same place is susceptible to wear; just resign yourself to replacing your thimble from time to time. Use thimbles that can be turned to distribute wear. This will delay, but not prevent the need for, replacement.
Favorite thimble has worn out.	When you find a comfortable, well-fitting thimble, buy two or three. (And keep them in a safe place so you can find them later when you need them!)
Inside of thimble is rusting.	To avoid corrosion on the interior of a metal thimble, wash and dry the thimble after each use.
Worn out thimbles are too pretty to throw away.	Keep your retired thimbles in a shadow box or special rack; in a few years it will be an impressive display.

Skill Builder

Your finger size can vary from day to day, even from hour to hour.

Finger size often depends on outside circumstances, like the weather (cold weather will sometimes make your fingers smaller; heat and humidity will make them a little larger) or on what you ate for dinner last night (salty foods can make your fingers swell). For quilting comfort, keep on hand thimbles that are one size smaller and one size larger than your ideal size. Many quilters have seasonal thimbles—one for summer and one for winter.

Try This!

Don't assume that one thimble is best for all of your stitching.

You may find that a thimble other than your quilting thimble makes your appliqué go much more easily, and still another kind works best for piecing. You may also need to change to a different thimble for different weights of fabric or batting, or when you are using threads that require a different stitching technique. Keep an open mind and test different thimbles to find the ones that can make your work easier.

Choosing the
Best Marker

Quilters are always looking for the perfect marking tool. Ultimately, this dream of a perfect marker is, like many dreams, the desire for a simple solution to a complex problem. The fact is that no single marking tool will fill every need. But this chapter is a start. Here you'll learn what each type of marker does best so you can make the best choice to fit your needs.

Getting Ready

Before you add any markings to your quilt top, think about what you're willing to do to remove them. To get rid of some markings, you must wash or soak the quilt in water. If you haven't already tested the fabrics for colorfastness, taking the plunge with a nearly completed quilt is a big gamble. Stick with a marker that doesn't need water to come out.

Each quilt presents its own set of characteristics in the form of fabric colors and prints, type of batting, and the amount and kind of quilting. You may have a favorite marker, but that doesn't automatically make it the best choice for every quilt. Run a test by making a sample sandwich using fabrics from the quilt and try out one or more markers. Since some pigments may become embedded in the quilting, quilt the sample, then remove the markings the way you would remove them from the quilt.

Most of the markers described are available at your local quilt shop. If you can't find them there, try quilting and sewing notion catalogs (see Resources on page 124), or general sewing-supply stores. Art supply stores are also good sources for some markers.

Marker Options

Graphite Pencils

Description: #3 or #4 hard lead pencils, mechanical models with .5 mm lead, ¼-inch-diameter graphite rods in a holder

Benefits: Mark uniformly, even over seams. These lines stay put, an advantage when you mark the entire quilt before quilting. Mechanical pencils never need sharpening.

Tips for using: Mark with a light hand. Easiest to use before the quilt is basted. Thin lines may be covered by the quilting stitches. Remove by washing the finished quilt or by rubbing lines with a fabric eraser. (See page 25 for some more tactics to try.)

Look for: Cottage Tools Treasure Marker graphite, Karisma Graphite Aquarelle, Ultimate Marking Pencil for Quilters

Markings made with #2 lead pencils may be too dark to remove easily and can smear on lighter fabrics.

Colored Pencils

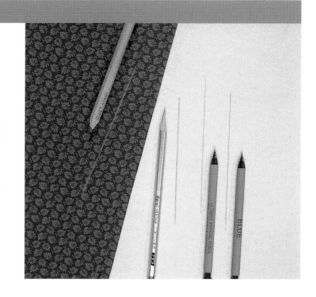

Description: Regular or mechanical pencils with colored leads

Benefits: White and colored pencils show well on dark or print fabrics. Silver works on light or dark fabrics.

Tips for using: Silver and white sharpen easily and hold a point. Thicker Dixon pencils need an extra-large or adjustable sharpener. Their soft lead needs frequent sharpening to hold a fine line.

Look for: Berol Verithin silver and white; Clover marking pencils (pink, blue, white, and yellow); Dixon pink, blue, and green; Ultimate Marking Pencil for Quilters with red, blue, and yellow leads

Tip

Yellow-color pencil marks can be especially difficult to remove, so be sure to test them first.

Chalk Markers

Description: Chalk markers come as pencils, triangular-shaped pieces of solid chalk, thick rods that fit in holders, or in wheeled dispensers.

Benefits: Available in a variety of colors to mark on all kinds of fabrics. Chalk usually removes easily by brushing or rubbing.

Tips for using: Markings may brush away as the quilt is handled. Most useful for marking as you quilt.

Look for: Clover Chaco-liner or Triangle Chalk, Cottage Tools Treasure Marker chalk, General's Multi-Pastel Chalks or Sketch and Wash pencil, Roxanne's Quilter's Choice pencils

Tip

Chalk wheel dispensers, such as Chaco-liners, mark a fine line with little drag.

Washout Markers

Description: Pens with blue water-soluble ink, in regular and fine point

Benefits: Easy to apply. Markings stay until they are removed with cold water.

Tips for using: Use them with a light hand. Mark with a dotted line rather than a solid one to use less ink. These markers should be used only *before* a quilt is basted; otherwise, the ink can soak into the batting, making removal more difficult.

Look for: Clotilde's Fine Tip Water Erasable pen, Collins Washable Wonder Marker, Quilter's Resource Water Erasable Fabric Marking Pen

Tip

In areas of high humidity, the marks made by water-soluble pens can disappear on their own.

Air Erasable Pens

24 hours old

Description: These pens leave a purple or pink mark that remains visible for 12 to 24 hours, fading completely in about 48 hours.
Benefits: The line is highly visible on light and most medium-value fabrics. They are useful for marking designs that will be quilted immediately.
Tips for using: Use only after basting, then wash the quilt after the quilting is completed to remove remaining traces of the chemical used.
Look for: Collins Vanishing Fabric Marker, Quilter's Mark-B-Gone Marking Pen or Quilter's Resource Air Erasable Fabric Marking Pen

Cold water removes the marks made by the air erasable pen more quickly.

Hera

Description: A hard plastic, palm-size tool with a thin edge. Applying pressure while drawing the hera across fabric creates a long-lasting indentation.
Benefits: Use before or after basting. The marks hold well on all fabrics and are visible on most except a dark, busy print.
Tips for using: Place unbasted quilt tops on a padded surface for marking. Use a rotary ruler as a guide. A hera can also be used with stencils and templates.
Look for: Clover Hera marker

Any unquilted markings made with a hera disappear when the quilt is washed or dampened with a cloth.

Needles

Description:. Darning needles (size 16–18), or 3½- or 5-inch doll needles make indentations in the fabric similar to the hera.
Benefits: Great for marking small designs. Mark before or after basting.
Tips for using: With the pointed end almost flat on the quilt, apply pressure and pull the needle across the fabric. Draw slowly to avoid dragging the fabric.
Look for: Clotilde's giant quill (technically not a needle, but works along the same principle), yarn darners, doll needles

Try a size 11 or 12 metal crochet hook in place of the needle. Its longer handle can provide better control.

Soap

Tip

For easier marking, put soap slivers in the refrigerator to harden.

Description: Slivers of soap (without cold cream) or soapstone pencils
Benefits: Soap slivers are inexpensive, readily available, and the marks come out easily. Soapstone comes as a long, thick rod that fits in a holder.
Tips for using: Most marks come out in the quilting process, but any that remain can be removed by rubbing lightly with a damp cloth.
Look for: Soap, EZ Soapstone pencils, Cottage Tools Treasure Marker

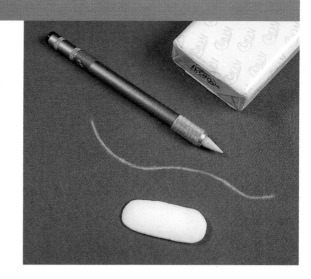

Tape

Tip

Leave a thread's width between the tape and the quilting so you can see and correct any crooked stitches before you remove the tape.

Description: Masking tape in a variety of widths can be applied to the quilt to provide stitching guides.
Benefits: Easy on and off for totally mark-free quilting. A fast way to guide straight lines or cross-hatching.
Tips for using: Always remove tape at the end of a stitching session to avoid sticky residue.
Look for: Painter's tape and masking tape. Tiger Tape comes in ⅛-, ¼-, and ½-inch widths with black lines to make 9 or 12 evenly spaced stitches per inch. The ⅛-inch width is flexible, making it perfect for curves.

Pouncing

Tip

To make a pouncing pattern, draw the quilting design on paper. Stitch along the lines with an unthreaded machine and a large (size 100) needle.

Description: Blue or white powdered chalk in holders or cloth bags is rubbed across the top of a stencil or quilting pattern with holes, leaving a pattern of lines or dots on the quilt.
Benefits: Simple to apply and remove.
Tips for using: Because the marks brush off so readily, use only after basting. Mark only about 12 inches ahead at a time.
Look for: Powdered chalk is commercially available, or use kitchen standbys like cornstarch and powdered cinnamon. To hold the powders, look for the Stencil House pouncer or the Quilter's Stencil transfer pad.

The Quilter's
Problem Solver

Making the Marks Go Away

Problem	Solution
Washout pen markings keep returning.	This usually occurs when marks have been removed by rubbing with a wet cloth, spraying, or dabbing. This dissipates the solution without removing it. Flush out the solution completely by soaking the quilt in a bathtub or washing machine filled with cold water. Unless you totally saturate the quilt, the marks will keep coming back, and the chemical used in the ink could damage the fabrics. It's a good idea to do this with the air erasable marking pens, too.
Pencil and chalk marks linger after quilting.	Try one of these treatments to remove the marks, but test your chosen method on a sample of your fabric before using on the quilt. ❏ Mix 6 drops of dishwashing liquid (not Dawn) with a solution of 1 ounce of water and 3 ounces of rubbing alcohol. Dab the mixture on the mark, then wash the quilt. ❏ Saturate the marks with inexpensive hair spray, then wash the quilt.

Skill Builder

Let the fabric "mark" itself.

Many print fabrics have motifs, color arrangements, or general patterns that can provide a guide for quilting without any additional marking from you. Just stitch around the patterns in the fabric. With a busy print, the quilting provides mainly texture; a specific pattern becomes less important. Use thread to match the fabric background so that the thread color doesn't distract from the texture you are creating.

Try This!

To remove pencil marks, look for an eraser made specifically for fabric at quilt shops or fabric stores.

Rub it back and forth across the marks, always rubbing with the grain of the fabric. For more control and an easier grip, look for pencil-shaped push-button fabric erasers like the Berol Quick-Erase. Or try an old white 100 percent cotton T-shirt. Rub the fabric in the direction of the lengthwise or crosswise grain. The soft cotton erases graphite beautifully with gentle rubbing.

CHOOSING THE BEST MARKER

Picking the
Best Batting

Gone are the days when a quiltmaker faced the labor-intensive task of carding and seeding cotton to use as filler for her quilts. Today's lucky quilters can select from a multitude of batts, in all sorts of fiber combinations, all neatly sized and packaged at the local quilt, craft, or fabric shop. Before you choose a batting, consider the characteristics described on the next page. Thinking through all these factors will make it easier for you to select the batting that is perfect for the kind of hand quilting you want to do and the finished look you're after.

Batting Basics

Bearding: All batts beard to some degree, meaning their fibers migrate to the outside of the quilt, creating a fuzz (or beard) on the front and back of the quilt. With natural fiber batts, this bearding usually disappears when you wash the quilt, but with many polyester batts, the fibers stick together and form little pills that are almost impossible to remove. Wool batts will also beard, but not as much as polyester.

Drape: Some battings result in quilts that are soft and snugly while others give a stiffer finished product. If you are making a wallhanging, the stiffer batt is the better choice, but if you want to sleep under the quilt, choose a softer one.

Loft: This term describes the amount of puffiness the quilt will have when it is completed. High loft batts are puffy; low loft ones are flat.

Needlepunching: This is a finishing technique in which batting fibers are punched with special needles to bind them together. These battings resist bearding and tend to be easier to hand quilt when they do not contain a scrim.

Needling ease: Needling describes how much pressure is required to push the needle through the quilt sandwich.

Scrim: Scrim is a lightweight, nonwoven material made of polyester or polypropylene threads. It may make a batting a bit harder to hand quilt, but the lines of stitching can generally be farther apart.

Batting Profiles

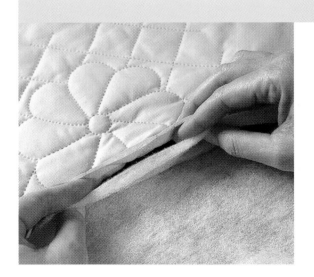

Polyester

Stitching interval: Up to 3 inches apart
Ease of needling: Easy
Final look and feel: Choose low loft for an antique look or to highlight your quilting stitches. Although a bit more difficult to hand quilt, the higher lofts give quilts more of a comforter feel and are also suitable for tying.
Preparation/care: No preshrinking needed. Since polyester holds up well to multiple washings, it is ideal for quilts that will get lots of wear.
Look for: Fairfield Low Loft, Hobbs Cloud Light, Mountain Mist Polyester

Tip

To prevent the backing fabric from shadowing through when using polyester batting, use a backing fabric no darker than the lightest fabric in the top.

100% Cotton

Stitching interval: Every ½ to 2 inches
Ease of needling: Moderate
Final look and feel: These low-loft batts drape and handle beautifully, finish flat, and show off stitching well.
Preparation/care: Most cotton batts, especially unbleached batts, can be presoaked to control shrinkage, but some brands cannot. Read package instructions carefully.
Look for: Fairfield Soft Touch, Hobbs Heirloom 100% Organic Cotton, Mountain Mist Blue Ribbon, Simply Cotton

Tip

Cotton batts that have any bits of seed hulls or leaves should be soaked to eliminate the chance that these natural elements could bleed onto light fabrics.

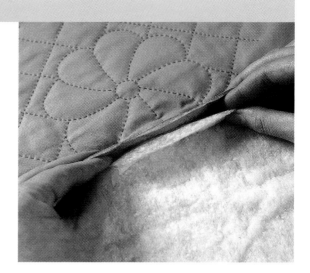

Cotton/Polyester Blends

Stitching interval: Every 2 to 4 inches
Ease of needling: Moderate, but easier if batting is presoaked.
Final look and feel: These low-loft batts have the appearance, drape, and feel of cotton. Blends are a popular choice for quiltmakers who favor the antique look.
Preparation/care: Blended batts should be preshrunk before they are used for hand quilting. Be sure to read the package instructions carefully.
Look for: Fairfield Cotton Classic, Hobbs Heirloom

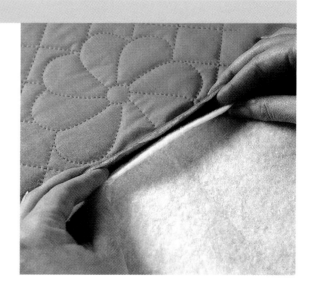

Wool

Stitching interval: Up to 3½ inches
Ease of needling: Easy
Final look and feel: Wool batts finish with a slightly puffy appearance, but drape well.
Preparation/care: Cleaning can often be handled at home. Like all wool products, however, quilts made with wool battings must be guarded against moth and other insect damage. Read the package instructions for specific care information.
Look for: Hobbs Washable Wool, Simply Wool, Warm and Natural Wool

Tip

It's best to use wool battings with light and medium color fabrics, as the bearding will show up on dark fabric.

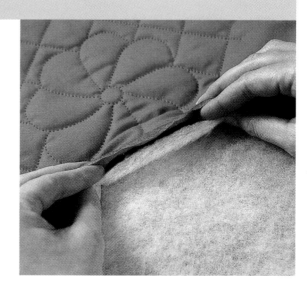

Stitching interval: Up to 10 inches
Ease of needling: Moderate
Final look and feel: Not quite as flat as cotton, but soft and supple after presoaking.
Preparation/care: Presoak in a mild detergent. Shrinkage is approximately 3 percent.
Look for: Perfect Harmony

Preparing the Batting

Preshrinking

Cotton/polyester blends should typically be preshrunk before being used. *Always* read the package instructions carefully to determine if pretreatment is required.

The easiest way to preshrink batting is to place it in a washing machine filled with warm water. Dunk the batting to make sure that it is completely soaked, with no dry spots. To avoid shredding the batt, *do not agitate the washer.* Drain the water, then use the spin cycle to remove excess moisture. Remove the batt carefully from the washer, and place in the dryer on the gentle cycle.

Banishing Wrinkles

Although preshrinking polyester batting is unnecessary, and presoaking is rarely—if ever—recommended, it may require some TLC before being basted into your quilt. The tight confines of its plastic packaging can compress the batting and create wrinkles and creases.

Never iron a polyester batt! Instead, remove it from its package two or three days before you plan to use it. **Spread it carefully over a bed,** then close the door to keep pets away. By the time you are ready to baste, the batting will be relaxed and wrinkle-free.

Tip

If planning ahead is not your strong suit, simply tumble crib- to queen-size polyester batts in a dryer set on air-dry for 5 to 10 minutes.

PICKING THE BEST BATTING

Joining Sections

1

Sometimes you will need to join sections of batting to get a large enough usable piece. Or you may be feeling thrifty and want to use up your batting scraps. **Cut the edges of the batting with a rotary cutter and ruler for the straightest lines.**

Overlap the edges of the batting about 1 inch and cut in the middle of the overlapped section. Carefully remove the trimmings, keeping the straight edges aligned.

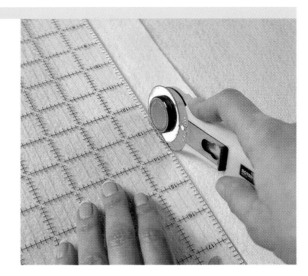

Tip

To keep the line straight when you move the ruler, leave the cutter in position. Butt the ruler against the cutter when you reposition it.

2

An alternative method for piecing batts is to cut the edges in curves or waves. Although this takes a little bit more effort, the seam is less noticeable in the finished quilt. **Overlap the two pieces of batting 2 to 3 inches. With a rotary cutter, make a series of gentle S-shapes, avoiding any sharp angles.** Be sure to cut through both layers at once to assure that you'll have matching edges. You can also use a pair of scissors, but you will need to be extra careful to make sure the layers don't shift during cutting. Pinning helps.

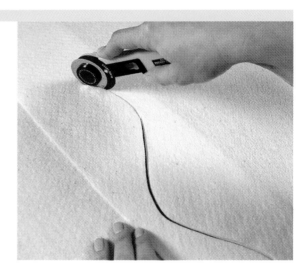

Tip

Save your old rotary blades and use them to cut batting, especially polyester. The batting tends to dull your blade more quickly.

3

Butt the edges closely together, avoiding any overlap. Overlapped edges create a lump that can mar the appearance of the quilt and cause trouble during quilting. **Join the pieces by hand with a simple whipstitch, cross-stitch, or herringbone stitch.**

Use a milliner's needle and white or off-white sewing thread. The milliner's needle is longer than a quilting needle and makes it easier to get a good bite of both sides of the batting. Pull the thread just tight enough to keep the pieces aligned, but not so tight that a wrinkle forms along the seam.

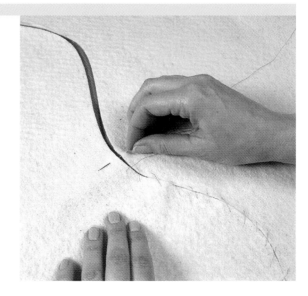

Tip

Always piece batting by hand. Machine stitching "squashes" the seam line, leaving a hard line that is obvious to the eye and difficult to quilt.

The Quilter's
Problem Solver

Beating the Bearding Blues

Problem	Solution
Batting fibers migrate through a quilt top, showing up after the quilting is completed.	While there's no easy fix for a completed quilt, avoid this problem in the future by choosing good-quality, tightly woven fabrics for your quilt tops and backings. Carefully follow any recommended batting pretreatment. Select a batting known for its resistance to bearding. For example, needlepunched battings may beard initially but tend to be quite stable over time. If you think bearding will be a problem, use dark-color batting in a quilt with predominantly dark fabrics, and a white or ecru batting with predominantly light-color quilt tops.
Bearding occurs most noticeably while you are stitching.	Try a different size or brand of needle, or a different thread. Often, a slightly larger needle will make a larger hole for the thread and eliminate the problem. Don't leave adhesive stencils or masking tape on your quilt for long periods of time. If you wax the quilting thread, iron it after waxing. Place the thread between two layers of paper towels to iron it.

Skill Builder

For a fun and informative guild program, try "Batting Practice."

Have the guild purchase or ask members to donate a half-dozen small (crib or craft size) battings of varying fiber contents and brands. Cut the batting into squares (12 to 14 inches) and sandwich each between two layers of muslin or solid-color cotton. Write the name of the batting right on the fabric. Baste three or four sandwiches with each batting, then pass the samples around. Members can quilt, compare, consult with their friends, and choose their favorites efficiently and inexpensively.

Try This!

Create a batting scrapbook.

As you finish each quilt, cut a small scrap of the leftover batting, and place it in a plastic notebook sleeve. Along with the batting, include the receipt (so you'll know where you bought it and what it cost); a note card describing your experience using that brand and type of batting; pretreatment, laundering, and care instructions; and—of course—a snapshot of the finished quilt. You'll have a handy reference when it's time to choose the batting for your next quilting project.

Basic
Quilting Styles

This chapter gives you a handy visual "vocabulary list" of the main types of quilting that have been used by quilters for generations. Glancing through the pages will help you decide which quilting will be right for your particular project. Accent quilting highlights the pieced or appliquéd shapes within the quilt, while background quilting fills open spaces. And in case you think that quilting is a once and done affair, see how progressive quilting can come to the rescue when the time available to quilt doesn't quite match the amount of stitching you'd like to add.

Getting Ready

One of the best ways to learn about different styles of quilting is by looking at quilts. Quilt shows, books, magazines, show-and-tell at your local guild—all of these places give you opportunities to view different quilting designs and see how they've been used. Train your eye to really study the stitching. Keep a notebook where you can collect quilting designs that appeal to you. When something catches your eye, you can draw a sketch of the quilting and add any notes describing what you like and how you might want to use it on one of your own quilts. Make it a habit to tuck this notebook into your tote bag or purse when you go on a quilting road trip to a shop, guild, or show. You never know when inspiration will strike. By collecting all these quilting styles and ideas in one place, you'll have a convenient resource when it comes time to decide what kind of quilting you want to do on your very own projects.

Accent Quilting

Outline Quilting

Quilting within a patch highlights that piece. **The time-honored approach is to simply outline the shape with a line of quilting ¼ inch from each seam.** If that doesn't provide enough quilting on large patches, add extra lines within the patch. Try dividing or repeating the shape, or inserting a motif that appears elsewhere in the quilt. Heavy quilting within the patch will flatten it, making it recede.

Use ¼-inch masking tape for the quickest and easiest way to mark. Or, practice eyeballing the spacing.

Ignoring the Seams

Not every seam needs to be outlined with quilting. Shapes in blocks are sometimes made of several patches. A quilting design that follows the larger shape, rather than the individual patches, reinforces the block design. **The diamond shape in the block shown is made of two triangles but is quilted as a diamond.** The quilting lines emphasize the larger unit and minimize the smaller shapes.

Quilting in the Ditch

Always a safe, reliable choice, quilting in the ditch is used to outline borders and sashing, and to define the shape of pieced and appliquéd shapes. Stitching in the ditch also serves to stabilize the areas for further quilting designs. **Place the line of quilting a needle's width from the seam line, away from the pressed seam allowance. Always stay on the "low" side of the seam.** When the seam allowance changes direction, change the side on which you stitch.

Background Quilting

Good Fillers

Background filler quilting is used in large open areas of pieced quilts and in appliqué quilts. It flattens the background and makes it recede to show off the pieced or appliquéd designs. **Traditional designs include cross-hatching with diagonal lines at 45 or 60 degree angles; double or triple diagonal lines that run parallel to each other; and chevron lines.** You can also use curved shapes such as a clamshell or hourglass.

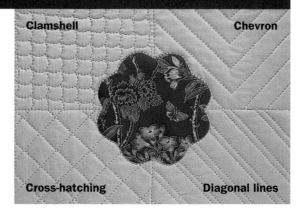

Clamshell   Chevron

Cross-hatching   Diagonal lines

Overall Quilting

Overall quilting covers the entire surface of the quilt, crossing over blocks, borders, and other units. It's equally suited to pieced and appliquéd quilts. Geometric designs are common, including parallel diagonal lines or cross-hatching. The overlapping Baptist fan pattern is another favorite. Overall quilting is a good choice to unify a quilt with diverse block patterns or many small pieces. It is a practical design for a utility quilt with many small pieces.

Tip

Remember that you must quilt through seam allowances when you use an overall pattern.

Echo Quilting

Echo quilting consists of multiple concentric lines of quilting that follow the outline of the design. The lines can be the same distance apart or the space between them can gradually increase. When echo quilting lines meet other echo lines, interesting new shapes are formed. You can then echo these new shapes with stitching. This type of quilting is used most often in the background of appliqué quilts. It is closely associated with Hawaiian quilts, where it covers both the background and the appliqué design.

Stipple Quilting

Stippling creates marvelous textured backgrounds. The random lines of wandering stitches that never cross, fill and flatten backgrounds and accentuate other quilting motifs like feathers. There are different styles of stippling. **Closely spaced lines that change direction frequently (A) create an appealing crinkly texture and pattern. Done in tight, echoed rows, stippling produces small uniform ridges (B). Opening up the spacing between the lines of stitching creates meander quilting (C).** Stippling is not marked, but instead "improvised" as you quilt.

Tip

Use the random, curved shapes of jigsaw puzzle pieces as your stippling inspiration.

BASIC QUILTING STYLES

Progressive Quilting

Stage A Quilting

Stage A quilting is the most basic stitching required to hold the layers of fabric and batting together so the quilt is usable. It can also stabilize the fabric sandwich for more quilting designs. Although some decorative designs may be present, Stage A quilting is most often simple outline quilting ¼ inch from a seam line or quilting in the ditch. You can bind your quilt after doing Stage A quilting and know that it has the basic minimum stitching it needs to stay together.

Stage B Quilting

Stage B quilting is more decorative and starts to fill in between the Stage A lines. **At this point, add motifs within larger shapes. Quilt the spaces between pieced or appliquéd motifs. Expand designs to fill large spaces, including borders.** Try to work the stitching uniformly over the entire quilt, although some areas with less quilting may be unavoidable.

Prize-Winning Quilting

Prize-winning quilting is notable for both the quality and quantity of stitching. The designs flow and fit the areas in which they are found, beautifully enhancing the pieced or appliquéd work. This is where you start to add elaborate feather, cable, or other decorative patterns. Turn single grid lines into doubles or triples. Don't leave any large, puffy, unquilted areas. The goal is to have each part of the quilt stitched at approximately the same density.

Changing Your Mind

Problem	Solution
Determining how a design will look before quilting.	Try one of these ways to audition your pattern before you commit it to stitches. Trace it on waxed paper or tracing paper and place it over the area. Stitch the pattern with large stitches (especially grids) and don't knot the thread ends. Mark the motif with a marker that you can easily see, but also easily remove if you don't like the pattern.
Removing hand quilting without leaving any telltale stitch holes or threads.	If there are holes left in the fabric after you have picked out the stitches, spritz the affected area with water (don't soak it, though). It will make the fibers in the fabric swell a little and minimize the holes. To remove telltale thread ends after you have unpicked stitches, roll a piece of masking tape around your hand with the sticky side out. Press the tape onto the threads; the tape will pick them up.

If you have made a quilt from a book, pattern, or magazine, here's a good way to get a sneak preview of your planned quilting design.

Place a plastic sheet protector over the diagram or photo of the quilt, then draw your quilting design on the plastic with a permanent pen (use one with an extra-fine point). Try several different designs. You can easily see the effect on the quilt through the plastic. If you have a color photo of your quilt, use that instead of the quilt drawing.

Try This!

For continuity of design, repeat motifs in several areas of the quilt.

For example, a heart shape quilted in a block can be repeated in the corner of borders, or it can be enlarged for side-setting and corner triangles of a diagonally set quilt. You can also place the motifs side by side for a border, or use four of them, rotating them around the center, for an alternating block. Enlarge or reduce the size as necessary to fit the design to the space you have.

"Quilt as Desired"
Finally Explained

Nothing drives quilters, especially beginners, to despair more than the phrase "quilt as desired." This vague phrase often accompanies project directions and leaves many a quilter staring at her quilt top wondering, "What exactly do I desire?" Not to worry—the next couple of pages give you lots of tips and guidelines that will steer you to the quilting designs that perfectly suit you and your quilt.

Getting Ready

To figure out what you "desire," start with this handy list of questions. Your answers will make it easy for you to figure out how much quilting you need to do and where you want to put it.

What kind of batting are you using? Check the packaging or the tips on pages 27 to 29 to see how close the lines of stitching need to be. Closer spacing means you'll need to fill more areas of the quilt.

How much time do you want to spend quilting? To get a quilt done faster, select the minimum amount of stitching you need to keep the layers together.

What part of the quilt do you want to be center stage? Elaborate quilting can sometimes overshadow the piecing or appliqué. Decide which element you want to shine and then either play up or play down the quilting.

How much marking are you interested in doing? If you're a minimalist, choose to add quilting in places where you won't have to mark.

How will you use the quilt? A utilitarian quilt (the kind your kids or grandkids snuggle under) doesn't need to be quilted to within an inch of its life—it needs just enough to hold the layers securely together. A quilt you're planning to display or enter in a show needs more quilting and lots of it.

Read on to find more guidelines that will help you determine exactly what kind of quilting you want to use.

The Fabric Factor

The fabrics in your quilt can help determine the best quilting designs to use. **Printed or dark fabrics make quilting designs disappear.** On these fabrics, choose a simple design like an overall pattern, outline, or in the ditch quilting. On medium- to large-scale prints, quilt around fabric motifs.

Reserve complex quilting designs for plain or light-color blocks. Quilting is much more visible on these fabrics and here it can be a focal point.

Patchwork Pointers

Tip

When quilting ¼" inside a patch, try curving the lines instead of making them straight.

Pieced quilts are typically made up of geometric shapes with straight lines and angles. **Pick a quilting design with curves to soften these angles and lines and provide a pleasing contrast to the piecing.** The feather pattern on the light side of the Perkiomen Valley Nine Patch block shows how effective this can be.

Straight-line quilting patterns accentuate the angles, lines, and points. For interest, try outline variations in the dark part of the block. Simple variations from horizontal and vertical quilting lines add interest and movement to ordinary piecing.

Accommodating Appliqué

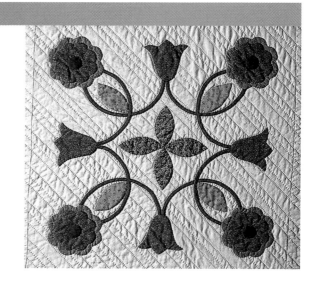

Tip

An undulating feather quilted on a border stands out against a quilted background of straight diagonal lines.

The rounded shapes of appliqué are beautifully set off by straight lines, especially ones that run diagonally behind the appliqué. The stitched background enhances the three-dimensional look of the appliqué. Echo the curves of appliqué in the sashing strip or border quilting by choosing curved patterns, such as cables or feathers.

Guided by Tradition

Here's a simple rule that will never let you down: match the quilting to the piecing. Traditional colors and pieced patterns work well with traditional quilting designs like cables, vines, flowers, and feathers. Geometric patterns give traditional patchwork a simple, clean, and timeless look. Stitching in the ditch and ¼-inch outlining are other time-honored choices.

Remember to provide a similar amount of quilting in all areas of the quilt. The unquilted areas will puff out and sag, and the batting in those areas will not hold up well to washing.

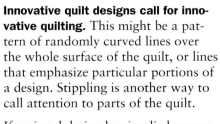

Innovative quilt designs call for innovative quilting. This might be a pattern of randomly curved lines over the whole surface of the quilt, or lines that emphasize particular portions of a design. Stippling is another way to call attention to parts of the quilt.

If a pieced design has implied curves (straight pieced seams that create the illusion of curves), adding curved-line quilting emphasizes the curved illusion.

Tip

Use a mix of curved and straight lines to add interest to the surface design created by your quilting.

Folk Designs

Fun and funky folk art quilts call for a casual approach to quilting. Elaborate, formal designs like feathers would look out of place, but a more casual adaptation of this design would work. Free-form quilting, where you quilt without any guidelines, plays along with the primitive, childlike nature of these quilts. Let go of your inhibitions and quilt an overall pattern like the clamshell totally by eye. Think of all the time you'll save by not having to mark!

Simple vs. Complex

Step back and take a look at the overall look of your quilt top. Is it simple or complex? **Choosing the opposite approach for the quilting design can make a good match.** Patchwork quilts with lots of small pieces or multiple prints benefit from simple quilting patterns that highlight the piecing. Simple patchwork, with large plain blocks (especially with light-color fabrics), gains from complex quilting patterns.

Tip

Repeat the same quilting motif in different ways throughout the quilt. Resize it or multiply it several times to fill an alternate block.

"QUILT AS DESIRED" FINALLY EXPLAINED

41

Designing Motifs
to Fit

Getting a good fit can be tricky business. Quilting books and magazines are filled with lots of appealing quilting designs, and there are scads of premade stencils in quilt shops. But more than likely the quilting motif you fall in love with won't be sized to suit the space you want to fill. Rather than abandon a motif that is too big or too small, use some of the tricks in this chapter to easily make it just right.

Getting Ready

Take a good look at the space you need to fill with a quilting design. If you have plain squares or alternating blocks, use a design that fills the space without leaving too much area unquilted and without crowding the motif in the block. Border designs need to fill the border width in the same way, filling the space adequately without crowding or being too narrow. Allow ¼ to 1 inch between the motif and the seam lines to make sure the design fills the space but still has enough breathing room. You can adapt the length to fit your quilt border by following the steps in this chapter.

▶ *See "Marking Made Easy" on page 48 for information on how to mark your design onto your quilt top.*

What You'll Need

- **Stencils or book of quilting patterns**
- **Tracing paper or freezer paper**
- **Waxed paper**
- **Template plastic or light-weight cardboard**
- **Fine-point permanent black marking pen**
- **X-Acto knife with double blade**
- **Paper punch**

Planning Designs

Sizing Motifs 1

The easiest way to change the size of a motif is to enlarge or reduce it on a copy machine. **If the design you want to resize is a stencil, trace the lines on paper first, then reduce or enlarge the tracing.** Determine the percentage difference between the original and the new size you want. For example, to enlarge a 6-inch design to 8 inches, enlarge the original to 133 percent (the 2-inch difference is one-third larger than the original 6-inch size, or 33 percent larger). Take the quilt with you to the copier, so you can audition different-sized motifs.

2

If the design is perfect except for a section that extends beyond the space you want to fill, try eliminating that section. You can draw new lines to reconnect the parts of the original design if necessary.

If your design doesn't quite fill the space and enlarging it doesn't work, add lines to fill the space, or combine elements of several designs to make your own custom pattern.

1 Fitting Borders

Border designs should flow evenly and turn corners gracefully. Most designs are made of repeated elements that form a pattern. The repeat size should fit all four borders equally. Measure the top and one side border. Determine a repeat size that fits both borders equally. If one fits perfectly and the other is just a little short or long (¼ inch or less), that's okay. You can fudge the placement of the motifs (see the next step).

Cut a piece of waxed paper the finished size of each border, including the corner. Fold it to match the repeat size. This is your master pattern.

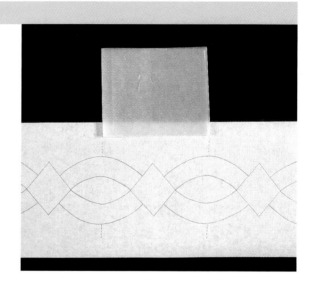

2

Tip

Don't worry about the corner yet, just draw the design across the whole length of waxed paper.

If the border design is symmetrical, trace the repeat on the top layer of the folded waxed paper. Press hard so the markings go through all the layers. **Unfold it to see the full border design.** If your design is asymmetrical, you must unfold the waxed paper and draw the entire border.

If one border repeat measurement is different from the other, fit the motif to the shorter repeat. **You can extend the motif on the longer repeat by lengthening some of the connecting lines.** The slight difference is not noticeable when it is spread out over the whole length of the border.

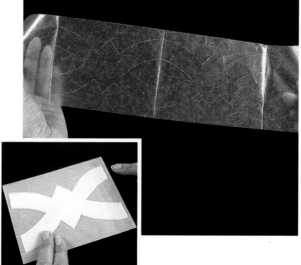
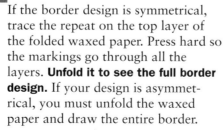

A mitered corner quilt design turns along a 45-degree line at each corner of the border. Cut a square of waxed paper the finished size of the corner; fold it in half diagonally. Choose a section of the border design to audition for the corner. **Place the folded square underneath that section, keeping the unfolded edges aligned with the edges of the master pattern.** Trace the pattern section onto the folded square. Unfold the paper to see the completed corner design. **Experiment with different areas of the border design to see which part makes the best corner.**

Tip

The borders themselves don't need to be mitered for this corner-quilting treatment.

2

There are two other ways to treat the corners. **Instead of making a border pattern flow around the corner, you can use a different motif in the corner.** The motif should relate to the border design in some way, and the border design should end gracefully at the corner.

If the border repeat is a freestanding motif, you can place one motif diagonally across the corner.

Tip

Look for stencils that include the corner treatment along with the borders. They might be available as single L-shaped stencils, or as two different stencils.

Customized Marking

Templates

Once you're satisfied with the border and corner designs, transfer them from waxed paper to either a template or stencil. Templates work well for individual motifs or designs that are made with single shapes like cables and pumpkin seeds. **To make a template, place a piece of template plastic on top of the waxed paper outline and trace one repeat motif. Cut along the outer and inner edges.** If the motif used in the corner is different, make a separate template for it.

Tip

Translucent template plastic lets you see through to the fabric, making placement easy.

DESIGNING MOTIFS TO FIT

Outline Stencils

Some quilt patterns translate nicely into stencils that are cut-out shapes, similar to the stencils used for painting designs on walls. Simple shapes that won't fall apart when the center is cut out work the best. **For blocks and side-setting pieces, from template material cut out a finished-size square or triangle. Inside this area, cut out the quilt pattern.** This makes positioning the design accurately on the quilt a breeze.

1 Channel Stencils

A channel stencil is a quilting pattern with narrow slots cut along the design lines. Small bridges between the slots keep the design in place. Slide a marker along the channels to transfer the design to your quilt top.

To prepare the channel stencil, trace your design onto the stencil material.

2

Place small marks on the plastic about every 2 inches to indicate where you will add bridges. **With an X-Acto double-bladed knife, cut along each line of the design, taking care to make smooth curves, straight lines, and sharp points.** Stop and lift the knife whenever you come to a marked bridge. When you have cut all the double lines, go back and carefully cut on each side of the bridges to trim the plastic away.

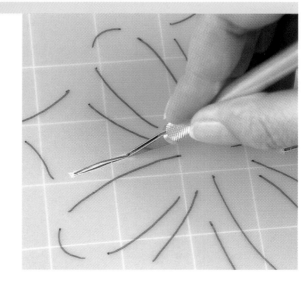

Missed Meetings

Problem	Solution
Border motifs don't quite meet in the center.	When marking a design, begin at the corners and work toward the center. Place registration marks along the border to indicate the beginning or ending of each repeat. If you line up the pattern with the registration marks before you trace it, the motifs should meet in the center. If they fall short by 1 inch or less, redraw the last two motifs, centering them in the expanded space and extending the lines that join them so they meet. If the gap is larger than 1 inch, remeasure the repeat, check the markings, and redraw the pattern.
Motifs overlap a little (1 inch or less) in the center.	Redraw the two motifs closest to the center, centering the repeat in the available space. Shorten the lines that connect the motifs, subtracting an equal amount from each side of each repeat.

Skill Builder

What do you do when you've found a motif you like but it doesn't quite look right or fill the space properly? Try one of these tricks to see if you can make it work.

❑ Rotate the design to see if it might work better placed at a different angle.

❑ Add a grid of 45 degree diagonal lines behind it.

❑ Echo quilt around it with several lines spaced about a finger width apart.

Try This!

To eliminate the two-step transfer of designs to tracing or waxed paper, then onto the stencil material, try cutting the stencil using a piece of glass as the cutting surface.

Tape the pattern to the glass with the right side facing the glass. Tape the stencil material on the other side of the glass. Cut along the lines with the double-bladed knife. If you have already traced the design onto the stencil material, use a rotary-cutting mat as your cutting surface.

DESIGNING MOTIFS TO FIT

Marking Made *Easy*

T he truth about marking is that you spend a lot of time doing something that ultimately you don't want anyone to see. But it's worth doing right. How you mark your quilt has a huge impact on how smoothly your quilting goes. Once you've selected a marker and quilting design, use this lesson for some hands-on help to transfer the design to your quilt top.

Getting Ready

The design you choose and the marker you decide to use are the starting points for determining *when* and *how* to mark. Design and marker will guide whether you mark the quilt top before or after it is layered and basted. The basic options are marking with the design underneath or with the design on top. If you are using a traced pattern, use the design-underneath method. Mark other patterns with the design on top. You'll need to decide whether to mark all at once or as you go. Some markers allow you to mark after the quilt is basted using the design-on-top method. To help you make the best decision, see the chart below.

When to Mark	Things to Consider
Mark before basting when:	You're sure you won't want to change the quilting design There's an elaborate design that needs precise placement You want to use a washout pen You're using a traced pattern that needs the design-underneath marking method
Mark after basting when:	You want to use the design-on-top marking method A hera or other pressure-marking tool will be used You want to use tape or other self-stick material
Mark all at once when:	You want the marking complete so that you can quilt uninterrupted You're definitely committed to the design; although changing is possible, it will be additional work The marker is relatively permanent and markings will hold up through handling
Mark as you go when:	You want freedom to change the design as the quilting progresses You're working with a stencil or template suited to the design-on-top marking method The markings rub off easily

Marking with the Design Underneath

1

In this method, a quilt tracing guide is placed underneath the quilt top and you trace the lines onto the fabric. It is most effective with a light source behind the tracing guide. This is the best method to use with intricate patterns like intertwined vines, and patterns that have a continuous line like cables and feathers.

Freezer paper makes the best quilt tracing guide, since it is easy to find and inexpensive and you can custom-tailor it to the size and shape of each area of your quilt.

2

To make a quilt tracing guide, cut a piece of freezer paper the exact size of the area on which you want to draw the design. Draw marks on the freezer paper for matching, such as a lengthwise line through the center of a border, or lengthwise, crosswise, and diagonal lines through a square. **Draw the design onto the freezer paper, centering it and aligning the sections as necessary.** Use a pencil and draw with a light line so you can revise the drawing if necessary. Go over the final drawn design with a black fine-point permanent marker.

3

Tip

Place the tracing guide on a white surface to make the lines more visible. White paper placed under the design works well.

Place corresponding matching marks on the quilt. Use pins, masking tape, or a basting stitch. To mark on light fabric, first secure the quilt tracing guide to a table or other flat surface. Place the quilt on the drawn design, aligning the registration marks. You can see through the light fabric to the design drawn on the freezer paper. Trace the quilting design on the quilt top with your chosen marker.

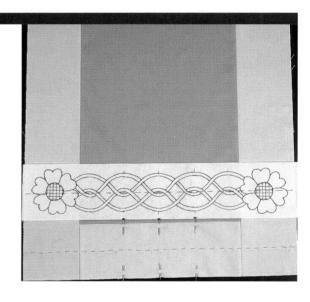

4

Tip

If your quilt is small, try taping the tracing guide and quilt top to a large window or a sliding glass door.

If you are marking onto dark or heavily patterned fabric, a light box makes tracing easier. For an inexpensive homemade light box, **purchase a translucent plastic storage box with a flat bottom (large thin ones work best) and an under-the-cabinet fluorescent light fixture. Turn the box upside down, place the light fixture underneath, and plug it in.** You can even cut out a place for the cord to come out underneath.

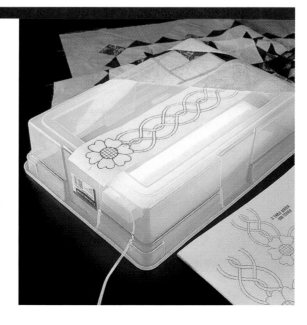

Marking with the Design on Top

In this method you place the marking guide (either a stencil or template) directly on the surface of the quilt top and trace through the stencil slots or around the template to mark the fabric.

Mark placement lines on the stencil. Mark similar lines on the quilt, especially the line dividing the border through the center. Using masking tape or painter's tape (from the hardware store), tape the stencil or template to the quilt, aligning the placement marks. Trace along the shapes with your chosen marker.

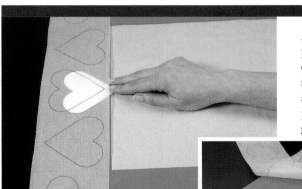

Adapt a technique developed by appliqué artists. Trace the quilting design on a piece of tracing paper that is the same size as the part of the quilt you are marking. Make templates of the parts of the design. (This is especially good for cables, vines, hearts, and other designs made from small repetitive motifs.) **Place the tracing paper over the quilt, aligning edges and centers, then carefully lift the tracing paper design and align the template underneath. Trace around the template with your chosen marker.**

Tip

This method works with both basted and unbasted quilts.

Smart Moves

Marking Single Blocks

Mark unpieced squares or setting triangles *before* you construct the quilt. **For triangles, draw a vertical line through the center of the design; add placement lines indicating the top of the fabric triangle.** Fold the fabric triangle in half; lightly press the center mark. Align the center markings and the top placement lines, secure the design to the fabric with tape, then trace.

Tip

To mark squares, align the center and both diagonals of the design with corresponding markings on the fabric.

MARKING MADE EASY

Line Thickness

Mark with the lightest possible line that you can still see. It is especially easy to mark too darkly if you are tracing with the light source behind the quilt top. Periodically lift the quilt top away from the light to double-check the thickness of the lines.

A good lamp to quilt by, preferably a portable task light that shines over the area you are working on, will help you see very light lines. Keep your stencil or drawn pattern close at hand—you can refer to it easily if the lines become too light to see.

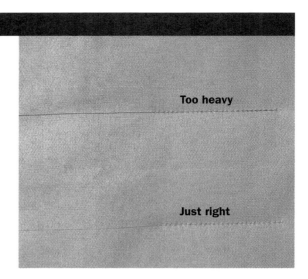

Dealing with Prints

Busy prints often cause visibility problems when you try to mark them. Test several different markers, remembering that you may need to use more than one kind of marker on the same fabric, depending on which area of the fabric you are marking. **If nothing else works, self-adhesive templates made from Con-Tact or sticky label paper are a good solution.** Quilt around the self-adhesive template. You may need to revise your design to use the templates, but it will probably be worth it.

Holding the Pencil

Tip

Use a regular pencil for this kind of marking. If you hold a mechanical pencil at this angle and press, the lead will break frequently.

The position of your pencil can cause drag on the fabric, especially if the point is very sharp. **Instead of holding the pencil upright, hold it at a 45 degree angle to the fabric.** In this position, it slides along smoothly without pulling on the fabric, and, as a bonus, you get a heavier line without pressing very hard. The pencil will also stay sharper longer.

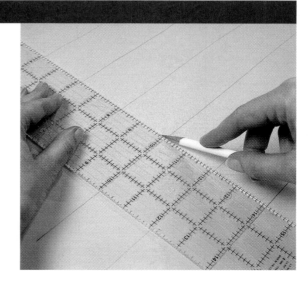

Tracing Patterns Accurately

Problem	Solution
Stencils or templates tend to slip out of place and distort the tracing.	Use drafting tape to hold patterns in place for tracing. It will remove easily without damaging the pattern, and it can be repositioned several times before the stickiness is gone. If you prefer not to tape a stencil or template to the quilt, use a paper punch to punch two holes in the pattern. Pin the pattern in position, placing the pin in one hole and out the other. Stick strips or dots of adhesive-backed sandpaper along the edges on the wrong side of stencils or templates.
Quilt slips on the marking surface.	Place the quilt on a tablecloth or a cutting mat to reduce the slipping and sliding that sometimes occur when you place a quilt on a smooth table or countertop for marking.

Make a friction board to help prevent the fabric from slipping when you are tracing patterns.

Using double-stick carpet tape, attach a piece of fine-grain sandpaper to a piece of heavy cardboard (like the back of a tablet), Masonite, or foam core board. To make a larger friction board, butt several pieces of sandpaper together. Make a square one for blocks and a longer one to use for borders.

Try This!

Use tulle netting or plastic needlepoint canvas to transfer a quilting design.

Enlarge or reduce the quilting pattern on a copy machine if necessary, then trace the design on the tulle or canvas with a Sharpie Fine Point marker. Trace over the pattern with a chalk marker or use the holes along the design to mark a dotted line on the quilt top. After removing the tulle or canvas, you may need to draw over the traced design with a sharp pencil to make a more distinct line.

Painless *Basting*

A sk any quilter to describe her favorite step in the quiltmaking process and it is highly unlikely you'll hear the word basting! *Although neither creative nor glamorous, a good basting technique is essential to the overall appearance of the finished quilt. For today's lucky quilter, basting is no longer synonymous with drudgery. In fact, with an ever-expanding selection of timesaving tools, and the assistance of a good buddy or two, the process of basting can be downright easy!*

Getting Ready

Before you baste, determine whether you'll be quilting in a hoop or a frame. With a hoop or a Q-Snap frame, baste your quilt as explained in this chapter. For another type of quilting frame, read "Installing a Quilt in a Frame" on page 68, since some frames require basting and others do not.

To prepare the quilt top, press it and snip any stray threads. Piece the backing if necessary, and press it. Review the batting directions to see if presoaking is necessary. Cut the batting at least 3 inches and the backing at least 6 inches larger than the quilt top.

Basting your quilt on a square or rectangular table is the easiest and best for your back. If the floor is your only option, wood, vinyl, and low-loft carpeting work the best.

In addition to the basting directions provided here, you may find the next chapter, "Back-Saving Basting Frame" on page 60, useful. It raises basting off the table or floor, helping you to save your back!

What You'll Need

- **Quilt top**
- **Batting**
- **Backing cut or pieced to size**
- **Table (Ping-Pong or office table)**
- **Masking tape**
- **Extra-long straight pins**
- **12 large binder or bulldog clips**
- **Milliner's or quilt-basting needles**
- **Neutral-color thread**
- **Thimble**
- **Spoon (optional)**
- **Embroidery scissors or thread snips**
- **Basting gun with tacking strips (optional)**

Layering the Quilt

Make sure that the basting surface is clean. Then measure the surface both horizontally and vertically. **Mark the midpoint along each side with a strip of masking tape.** These markings will guide you in centering the backing, batting, and quilt top.

Next, fold the quilt top vertically and horizontally to find the midpoint on each of its four sides. Finger press a crease to mark each midpoint. Repeat to find the midpoints of the batting and backing. If it's hard to see the creases, use pins to identify these key points.

An expandable work surface, such as a Create-A-Space folding table, is smooth and spacious—and the perfect height for basting in comfort.

2

Center the quilt backing wrong side up on the basting surface, using the marked midpoints and the surface markings as a guide. **Tape or clip the edges of the backing to the edges of the work surface.** Be sure that any seams are straight, and that the edges are parallel to the edges of the basting surface. Pull the backing taut so that there are no wrinkles or puckers, but be careful not to stretch the fabric.

If the quilt is larger than your work surface, refer to Step 5 on page 58 for instructions on basting a large quilt in sections.

3

Center the batting over the backing, again using the midpoints and the sur-face markings to guide you. **Working from the center out, gently pat out any wrinkles or folds so that the batting is flat and smooth.** Don't pull or tug. This may cause the batting to tear, or the backing to shift, pleat, or pucker.

In a similar fashion, layer the quilt top right side up over the batting and backing, making sure that the backing edges and seams align with those of the top. Again, work from the center of the quilt top, gently smoothing any wrinkles.

Thread Basting

1

Before thread basting, secure the layers with straight pins to keep them from shifting. Specially made quilter's pins are ideal for quick, efficient pin bast-ing. Long shafts allow them to glide through three bulky layers, while col-ored plastic heads make them easy to see and remove when the job is done.

Always pin from the center outward. Pin first in a vertical, then a horizontal line from the center of the quilt, smoothing gently as you go. **Next, work your way to the quilt's edges by pinning each quadrant at 6-inch intervals.**

2

A milliner's or quilt-basting needle makes the entire basting process go more quickly and efficiently. Each is long, fine, sharp, and has a large eye for easy threading. Avoid needles designed for embroidery, cross-stitch, or crewel work. Although large, they have thick shafts and blunted tips that leave visible holes in the quilt top where the needle pierces the fabric.

Use white or beige medium-weight cotton or cotton-wrapped polyester thread for basting. Skip dark threads for basting that may leave dots of dye in lighter fabrics when basting stitches are removed.

3

Once the quilt is securely pinned, thread baste it. Thread the needle, but don't cut the thread off the spool. **Baste from one edge to the opposite edge.** Pull the thread along as you work. If your quilt is very large and it becomes difficult to pull the thread, take a backstitch and cut the thread from the spool. There is no need to knot it. When you finish the first line, take a backstitch, then cut the thread, leaving a 6-inch-long tail.

Baste in parallel lines 4 inches apart both horizontally and vertically across the quilt.

Tip

Use a spoon to spare your fingertips. The tip of the spoon guides the needle tip up through the layers.

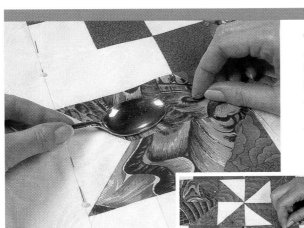

4

Traditional basting is done with an oversized running stitch—as long as 2 inches on the top of the quilt, and 1 inch underneath. Be sure to use enough stitches to secure the layers.

A zigzag or tailor's basting stitch is an alternate method. Begin at the center of the quilt and take a horizontal stitch about 1 inch long. **Drop down about 2 inches below where the first stitch began and take another horizontal stitch.** Continue until you have reached the edge of the quilt, finishing with a backstitch. The horizontal stitches will be on the back of the quilt, while long diagonal stitches appear on the top.

Tip

Constant rubbing of the needle against your thumb can cause a painful blister. Cover it with a piece of moleskin for protection.

5

If you are basting on a table that is smaller than the quilt top, you will need to move the partially basted quilt to complete the basting process. **Start basting from the center and move outward, leaving the lines of basting unfinished, with thread dangling over the table's edge.** Remove the clips or masking tape holding the layers to the surface, and carefully slide the quilt until you have exposed the next area to be basted. **Replace the clips or tape to secure all three layers, rethread, and continue basting.** Remove all pins when you have finished thread basting.

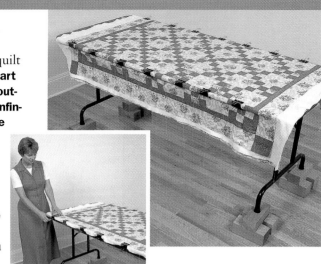

Basting Gun

1

Tip

Save safety pin basting for machine quilting. It's too easy to catch a pin on the hoop and tear the quilt top or the backing.

A quilt basting gun can cut basting time in half. A basting gun injects tiny plastic tacks to secure the top, batting, and backing into a tidy quilt sandwich. The tacks are small, lightweight, and flexible enough to be used with a quilting hoop or a quilting frame.

Layer and pin the quilt sandwich as for thread basting. **Beginning in the center, tack along the horizontal and vertical lines first, then work outward in a grid pattern, basting no farther apart than the width of your fist.**

2

Tip

Retape or reclip the quilt backing as you work your way around the quilt.

It's much easier to use a basting gun when the quilt is raised above the table surface. **Remove a section of tape or a clip so you can slide a tacking grid under the quilt backing.** If your quilt is large and you can't reach the center, the basting grid comes with long strings that can be used to pull it in any direction to reposition it. **When the grid is in position, poke the needle of the gun straight through all three layers.** Squeeze the handle quickly and release.

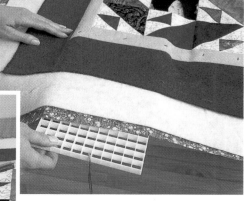

Puckers & Pleats on the Back

Problem	Solution
The backing of your basted quilt has bubbles and wrinkles when you remove it from the basting surface.	Sorry, there's no easy fix. This fullness in the backing won't quilt out. Take out the basting from the section that is bubbled and redo it. Keep the problem from recurring by following this checklist for better basting: ❏ Neatly press the backing before you begin basting. ❏ Have a friend or family member help you "layer the sandwich" so the backing doesn't shift in the process. ❏ Tape, clamp, pin, or otherwise anchor the backing to the basting surface. *Do not* skip this important step. ❏ Avoid sliding your free hand under the quilt to gather it while basting. ❏ Always smooth, pin, and baste from the center of the quilt toward the outer edges. ❏ Baste generously!

Skill Builder

To protect the "raw" edges of your quilt throughout the entire quilting process, try this finishing technique.

Finish basting with a single row of stitching around the perimeter of the quilt top. Fold the excess batting and backing over the raw edge of the top, trimming if necessary to keep the bulk down. Baste the edges firmly in place. Release the "hem" as your quilting approaches the edges of the quilt.

Try This!

To save your back when basting on a table, raise the table to your level with easy-to-build extender blocks.

For each block, cut three pieces of 4 × 4-inch lumber, each about 8 inches long. Attach one piece to each end of the third piece using glue and screws or nails. In the top of each extender, drill a ½-inch-deep hole that is just slightly larger than the diameter of the table leg. Place an extender under each table leg.

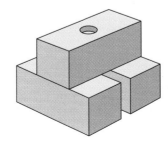

PAINLESS BASTING

Back-Saving
Basting Frame

T he good news about basting is that you're entering the homestretch and a finished quilt will soon be yours. The bad news is the backache involved. If you've ever spent hours crawling around on a hard floor or leaning over a table that's too low, this simple and inexpensive basting frame is your salvation. With just a little time, using easy-to-find materials, you can customize the height of the frame to get yourself up off the floor and ease the strain of basting a quilt.

Getting Ready

Sand the boards so they are smooth and free of splinters. Seal the boards with a coat of varnish or polyurethane to keep them clean and smooth, especially if you plan to use them more than once.

Clear space in a room that is big enough to handle the boards and leave enough room to walk around them. If none of the rooms in your house are big enough, try laying large plastic tarps on a garage floor to get enough room. You might also be able to use a quilt shop classroom if there is no class in session, or even a room in a church.

What You'll Need

Sandpaper

Four 1 × 3 boards, 10' long

Varnish or polyurethane

6" or larger square rotary ruler

Four C-clamps

A partner to work with you (optional but highly recommended)

30 (or more) bulldog clips or large binder-style clamps to fit over the edge of the boards

1

Lay the quilt backing, wrong side up, in the space where you will assemble the quilt frame. **Place the boards at right angles to each other on top of the backing, allowing the backing to extend about 2 inches beyond the boards on all sides.** This will allow room for the backing to be clamped to the edges of the boards. (The backing should be at least 3 inches larger than the quilt top all the way around.)

2

Use a square rotary ruler to make sure the corners are each 90 degrees. Clamp each corner firmly with a C-clamp. You will need a partner for this step, because it is almost impossible to make each corner accurate without help. If you can find three friends to help, that's even better. Having one person per corner makes it much easier to get the boards square.

Tip

Place a short stack of books under each corner to make it easier to get the clamps on the boards.

3

Rest the frame on the backs of four chairs, one at each corner. High-back chairs work really well for this, as they provide a comfortable height at which to work. Sawhorses or TV trays can also serve as supports. Make sure you have enough room to walk all around the frame.

Tip

For extra security, tie the frame to the chairs with strips of scrap fabric.

4

With the frame securely balanced on the supports, place the backing over the frame. **Pull the backing taut, but don't stretch it, and attach it to each side of the frame. Secure it in place with the bulldog clips or binder clamps.** Attach one side, then work on the opposite side; repeat for the two remaining sides. Working opposite a partner makes this step easier.

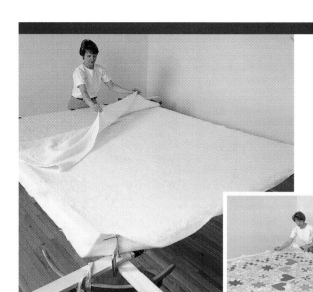

5

Spread the batting evenly over the backing and gently smooth it in place. Be sure to get all the wrinkles out, and take care not to stretch it. **Spread the quilt top over the batting and smooth it in place.**

6

Releasing one clamp at a time, gently pull the batting to join the backing, then reclamp both backing and batting to the frame. Be careful not to catch the quilt top in the clamp; this will remain free as you baste. Now you can stitch, pin, or tack your layers together with the quilt at a comfortable height.

7

To reach the center of a large quilt, baste as far as you can around the sides, then remove the frame from the chair supports and lean it against a wall. You can easily reach the center of the quilt to complete the basting. Turn the frame around if necessary to reach all the sections.

The Inside Scoop
on Hoops

Lap hoops are made for cozy quilting. With your quilt securely snugged into a hoop, you can curl up in a comfortable chair and be lulled by the soothing rhythm of your stitching. Because a hoop is portable, you can stitch wherever the spirit moves you— by the fire, next to a sunlit window, out on the front porch swing, or in the car on a long road trip. From bed size to wall size, any quilt can be beautifully stitched in a hoop.

Getting Ready

Your comfort is the primary goal when choosing a quilt hoop. Hoop sizes range from 10 to 22 inches in diameter; 14- to 18-inch hoops are the easiest for most people to use. Be sure you can reach your supporting arm around the hoop without straining. Also check the weight; the lighter the hoop, the longer you can comfortably quilt. Be sure to purchase a quilting hoop and not an embroidery hoop. Quilting hoops are 1 to 1½ inches deep and have slightly rounded edges; embroidery hoops are only about ½ inch deep and have sharper edges.

PVC pipe frames, commonly known as Q-Snap frames, are available as squares and rectangles and come in several sizes, including a floor frame.

Specialty hoops, such as D-hoops, are used to quilt the edges of a quilt.

What You'll Need

Quilt hoop, Q-Snap frame, or D-hoop

Basted quilt

Terry cloth hand towel

Using a Round Hoop

Separate the rings of the hoop. Place the bottom ring (without the screw) on a firm surface, such as a table. **Place the basted quilt over the bottom ring, then slide the top ring down over the bottom ring.** Tighten the screw just enough so there is some tension but you can still move the quilt in the hoop. **Turn the quilt over and look at it from the back, checking to be sure there are no wrinkles in the quilt.** If there are, gently tug the quilt to smooth them out.

Tip

Place the center of the quilt on the hoop first; when you have quilted the center, move toward the sides.

2

If you need to tug the sides of the quilt to straighten it in the hoop and remove wrinkles, always tug with the straight grain of the fabric. Tugging along the bias grain will stretch the quilt out of shape. This is especially important if your quilt is set diagonally, because the vertical and horizontal planes of the quilt are already on the bias.

Tip

A slack quilt should look like you put your sewing basket on it and the quilt sank a little under the weight.

3

If you use the rocking stitch to quilt, loosen the tension on the quilt. This allows you to manipulate the needle more easily without bending or breaking it and results in more even stitches. **Place the quilt and hoop on a tabletop and push down slightly on the top of the quilt to create a little slack.** Tighten the screw to securely hold the quilt.

For stab stitching, the quilt should be fairly tight in the hoop. If you need to tighten it, gently tug on the quilt just outside the hoop; tug with the grain of the fabric.

Tip

Look for a hoop on a floor stand; you can stitch with both hands free and position the hoop for the most comfortable stitching angle.

4

Position yourself so that both your hands are free to stitch. Both hands have important jobs to do; they can't do them if you are trying to balance a hoop in the crook of your arm. **Sit in a comfortable armchair and balance the hoop between your lap and the arm of the chair.** Another alternative is to sit at a table and balance the hoop between your lap and the edge of the table.

To maintain even tension when you get to the edge of the quilt, **try pinning or basting a terry cloth hand towel along the edge.** This way you can extend the edge of the quilt so it fits into the hoop properly, yet you can comfortably quilt right to the edge. Simply reposition the towel as you complete each section.

Using a Q-Snap Frame

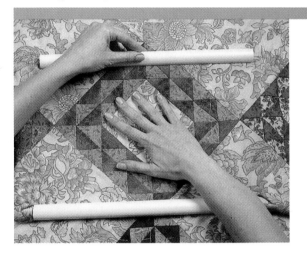

To arrange the quilt in a Q-Snap frame, remove the clamps from the sides of the frame. Place the center of the quilt over the bottom part of the frame. **Put a clamp on one side of the frame. Press your hand on the quilt in the center of the frame, then secure a clamp to the opposite side of the frame.** Repeat the process for the remaining sides of the frame. Holding the quilt down with your hand helps prevent the quilt from being too tight in the frame. Adjust the tension by rolling the clamps in or out.

Tip

With a new Q-Snap frame, the clamps will be fairly stiff and tight. They will loosen over time.

Using a D-Hoop

A D-hoop is round on one side and straight on the other; a fabric strip is attached to the straight edge. The hoop maintains even tension out to the edges of a quilt, ensuring smooth, pucker-free quilting. The round side opens like a mouth; one ring is smaller than the other. **To use, open the hoop and place the quilt on the smaller ring; the raw edges should be against the straight side of the hoop.** Pin the edge of the quilt to the fabric strip, then close the hoop. Check for wrinkles. Reposition as needed to work along the outside edges of the quilt.

Tip

Some D-hoops have tension screws; others rely on the pressure of the bent bars to keep the quilt under tension.

Installing a Quilt
in a Frame

Quilting in a frame is the traditional, old-fashioned way to quilt. The frame is the hub of the quilting bee, where lots of friends all work on the same quilt together. Although space for a floor frame may be at a premium in your home, if you can find the room, you'll love the convenience of having your quilt set up and ready to stitch whenever you have some free time.

Getting Ready

There are three kinds of floor frames: simple stretcher, two-rail roller, and three-rail roller. This chapter covers the two- and three-rail roller frames.

If you are using the two-rail frame, baste the quilt first with your choice of pins, quilt tacking gun, or thread. Make sure the backing is 3 to 4 inches longer than the quilt and batting on the ends that will fasten to the frame.

Three-rail roller frames are a recent labor-saving invention. You don't need to baste the quilt before installing it in the frame. Simply attach the layers to the proper rails and roll them up. The separate rails maintain an even tension as you roll the layers. Cut the backing and batting at least 6 inches longer than the quilt and at least 4 inches wider.

Two-Rail Frame

1

Measure each long rail and mark the center on all four sides with permanent marker. Find and mark the center of the two edges of the quilt that will be attached to the rails.

Match the center of the quilt to the center of the back rail (the one with the gears) and thumbtack it in place. Use regular thumbtacks, not push pins, which have larger heads. Tack the remainder of the quilt along the rail, being careful not to stretch it. Place thumbtacks about 4 to 6 inches apart. Tack the opposite edge to the front rail in the same manner.

Tip

Instead of thumbtacking, stitch the quilt to fabric strips, called leaders, that are stapled to the rails. See "The Quilter's Problem Solver" on page 73 for details.

INSTALLING A QUILT IN A FRAME

2

Tip

If you start at the back of the quilt and quilt toward the front, the bulk of the quilt will decrease as you stitch.

You can begin quilting at either end of the quilt, but if you have long continuous border designs, it's best to begin where the quilt is tacked to the back roller and quilt toward yourself. **Roll the quilt *under* and around the front roller.** Make sure the quilt stays straight in the frame, and smooth out any wrinkles by gently pulling on the sides. Roll the quilt as tight as you can, so you can reach over the bulk of the roll.

3

Tip

The S shape of the rolled quilt helps keep the tension even along the entire quilt.

Place the front rail in the middle slot on the side bars. **Roll the quilt around the back roller just enough to tighten it securely, making sure that the whole area at the top of the quilt is accessible for stitching.** Quilt the section of the quilt between the front and back rails.

To roll the quilt to expose the next section, lift the front rail out of the slot, and unwind the quilt enough so the rail will fit into the front slot. Roll the quilt *over* the back rail until it is tight. Secure the gears in the stoppers to keep the quilt taut.

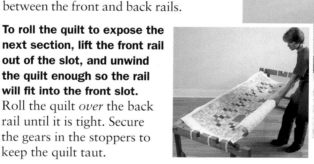

4

To keep the quilt taut from side to side, use spring clamps from the local hardware store. Cut six pieces of hook-and-loop tape, each about 24 inches long. **Poke a hole through the cover of the handle of the spring clamp. Thread a bolt through the hole and attach the loop side of the tape. Staple the hook side of the tape around the side rail of the quilt frame. Attach the mouth of the clamp to the side of the quilt and secure its tail to the quilt frame.** Adjust the tension on the tails as necessary.

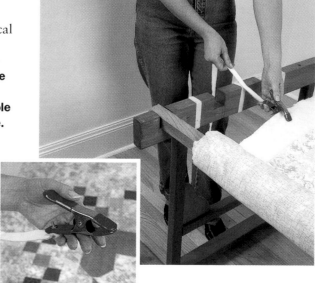

Three-Rail Frame

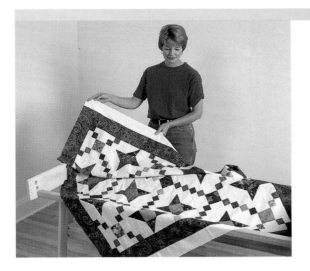

1 Machine stitch a 3-inch-wide strip of muslin to the two edges of the quilt that you will secure to the quilt frame, using a ¼-inch seam allowance. **These strips attach to the frame and will allow you to stitch all the way to the edge of the quilt.**

Check the backing and batting to make sure the top and bottom edges of both are straight and even, trimming as necessary to straighten.

2 **Find and mark the center of each of the three rails.** Mark each rail on all four sides with a pencil or a permanent marker.

Fold the quilt in half lengthwise to find the center of the top and bottom edges. Place pins at the folds. Find and mark the centers of the backing and batting in the same way.

3 Match the center of the top edge of the quilt backing with the center of the middle rail. Align the straight edge of the backing with the edge of the rail. Thumbtack the backing to the rail, placing the thumbtacks every 4 inches along the edge. **Attach the bottom edge of the backing to the front rail in the same manner.**

Roll the backing around the middle rail, making sure it rolls straight and evenly. Smooth out any wrinkles that develop as you roll. If smoothing doesn't work, unroll the backing and roll it again to keep it straight and wrinkle-free.

Tip

To make sure the backing rolls evenly, place a piece of masking tape on each end of the middle rail to mark the edge of the backing.

Tip

Use a spoon to remove the thumbtacks that attach the quilt to the rails. This trick will save your fingernails.

4

Align the bottom edge of the batting along the front rail, matching the center of the batting to the center of the rail. **Tack it in place, using the same thumbtacks that you used to hold the backing in place.** Drape the batting over the middle rail and between the middle and back rails. Some three-rail frames, like the Grace frame shown here, have an extra rail around which you can roll the excess batting. **Tack the top edge of the batting to this fourth rail and roll it around the rail.** Don't stretch it as you roll it on the rail.

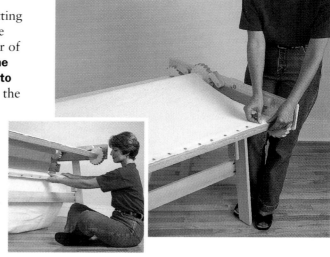

5

Attach the top edge of the quilt top to the back rail with thumbtacks, matching the center of the quilt to the center of the rail. Roll it onto the rail, keeping it even and smooth. **Unroll enough of the quilt to reach the front rail and thumbtack it in place with the backing and batting.** Use the same thumbtacks.

Tighten the quilt top around the back rail, keeping it smooth and straight, then secure the rail in the gear.

Tip

To shed more light on your quilt, place a swing-arm lamp in a hole drilled on each side of the frame.

6

When you have finished quilting the first section, release the middle and back rails and roll the quilted section onto the front rail. Tighten the backing and quilt top on their respective rails, then secure them in their gears. Make sure that the layers stay straight and unwrinkled. Repeat these steps each time you finish quilting a section.

The Quilter's
Problem Solver

Making Room to Maneuver

Problem	Solution

It's awkward quilting right next to the rail. Your hand can't maneuver the needle comfortably when the portion to be quilted is snugged up against the wood.

Add strips of fabric, called leaders, to each rail. These attach the quilt to the frame, while leaving enough free area for your hand to stitch out to the very edge of the quilt. You can use mattress ticking, canvas, or muslin. The advantage of mattress ticking is that when you cut it lengthwise, a straight line to align your quilt is built into the fabric.

Tear a 12-inch-wide piece of fabric along the lengthwise grain (tearing it keeps it on grain). It should be the length of the quilt frame rails. Fold it in half lengthwise and serge or zigzag stitch over the raw edges. Staple the serged edge to the rail with the folded edge facing the center of the frame. Place staples every 1 to 2 inches along the length of the rail. Pin or stitch the quilt layers to the leader rather than directly to the rail.

Skill Builder

Even with the most careful preparation, sometimes the quilt doesn't roll straight onto the rails.

It's easiest to fix if you have two people to help you roll. First, unroll the quilt back to where it is straight. While one person rolls each end of the rail, the third person maneuvers the uneven section onto the frame by pushing the full part under the rail. Roll slowly, putting extra tension on the full section until the quilt is straight again.

Try This!

Instead of spring clamps, use fabric strips to keep the quilt taut in the frame.

Cut two strips of fabric 1½ inches wide by 40 inches long. Pin one end to the leading edge on one side of the quilt. Wind it back around the quilt frame, then back to the quilt about 6 inches ahead of the first pin. Pin the strip to the quilt, then wind it around the frame again. Continue pinning and winding along the entire length, then repeat with the second strip on the other side.

INSTALLING A QUILT IN A FRAME

73

Starting, Stopping, and Sliding

Think back to when you were first learning how to drive a car. There were three basic things you had to master—accelerating, braking, and parking. No matter where you drive, you always need to be able to start, stop, and park. The same holds true for quilting. No matter what kind of quilting you're going to do, you'll need to know how to start, stop, and move the needle from one part of the design to the other.

Getting Ready

At times, the hardest part of getting ready to quilt is threading the tiny betweens needles. A needle threader can be your salvation. Poke the diamond-shaped wire of the threader through the needle's eye. Insert the thread into the open wire. Gently pull the thread-filled wire back through the needle. Don't pull too hard, though, or the threader might break. The Clover needle threader is particularly durable and has twin wires suited to small- and large-eye needles.

Basted quilt

Quilt hoop or frame

Betweens needles

Quilting thread

Needle threader

Thimble

Embroidery scissors or thread snips

Cake of beeswax (optional)

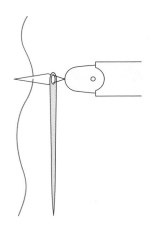

Starting

1

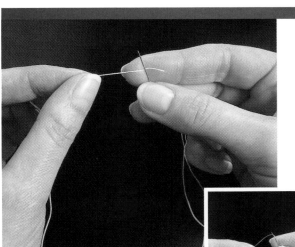

Thread the needle with an 18-inch length of thread. Longer ones tend to tangle and wear out at the needle's eye. To anchor your quilting stitches, you'll need to securely knot one end. **For an effective quilter's knot, hold the needle point up and overlap the thread to form a cross. Hold the "cross" in place with your thumb and forefinger as you wrap the thread *loop* (not the tail) around the needle two or three times.**

To visualize the knotting motion, imagine you're making a French knot in the air.

STARTING, STOPPING, AND SLIDING

2

Pinch the wrapped thread securely with your thumb and forefinger, then use your free hand to pull the needle through your fingers and the wrapped thread. Continue pinching the knot until it has traveled to the end of the thread. With practice, you'll be able to make the knot in a second or two without even thinking.

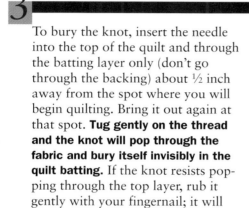

3

Tip

If the knot refuses to pop, it is probably too big. Cut it off and make another one. Two or three wraps are plenty.

To bury the knot, insert the needle into the top of the quilt and through the batting layer only (don't go through the backing) about ½ inch away from the spot where you will begin quilting. Bring it out again at that spot. **Tug gently on the thread and the knot will pop through the fabric and bury itself invisibly in the quilt batting.** If the knot resists popping through the top layer, rub it gently with your fingernail; it will usually go through.

4

Tip

If you prefer to clip the tail, follow the pointers in Step 3 under "Stopping."

If the thread tail sticks out on the surface of the quilt, insert the needle between the top of the quilt and the batting. **Point the needle toward the thread tail and sweep it around between the layers.** It will catch the thread and pull the tail through to the batting layer.

Stopping

You'll need to stop stitching when the thread remaining in your needle is about 6 inches long or when you reach the end of your line of quilting (whichever comes first). Don't wait until the thread is too short, or you will have difficulty tying off.

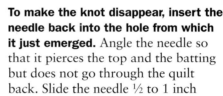

To make the ending knot, hold the thread toward you with your left hand (lefties, use your right hand). **Place the needle over the thread, then sweep it from left to right, catching the thread with your needle. Loop the thread tail twice over the needle in a counterclockwise direction.** Keep holding the thread in your left hand.

2

To make the knot disappear, insert the needle back into the hole from which it just emerged. Angle the needle so that it pierces the top and the batting but does not go through the quilt back. Slide the needle ½ to 1 inch forward, and bring it back to the quilt top.

Grasp the thread firmly with thumb and forefinger, close to the surface of the quilt. Tug gently. The loops will form a knot that pops through the quilt top and buries itself invisibly in the batting.

As with the beginning knot, no trace of the thread's tail should remain visible. **Firmly grasp the thread between thumb and forefinger, close to the quilt top. Pull the thread up and away from the quilt.** Don't pull *too* tightly or you'll affect the tension in the last few quilting stitches.

Use embroidery scissors or thread snips to clip the thread close to the quilt top, taking care not to snip the quilt in the process.

Tip

If you tugged too tightly, and the last few stitches have pulled up, run your fingernail gently along the stitched line to even out the tension.

STARTING, STOPPING, AND SLIDING

Sliding

1

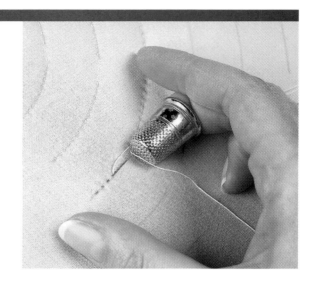

Occasionally you come to the end of a line of quilting with lots of thread still on the needle. You may wish to move to a nearby line and continue quilting, without the bother of tying off and beginning again. When quilting some designs, like feathers, you may need to move between areas that are not directly connected as a regular part of stitching.

If the area to cover is less than 2 inches, you can travel the distance with a technique called *sliding*. Other names for this technique include *jumping*, *floating*, and *traveling*.

Tip

Sliding is *not* a good idea when you are using dark quilting thread on a light background fabric. The long sliding stitch may show through.

2

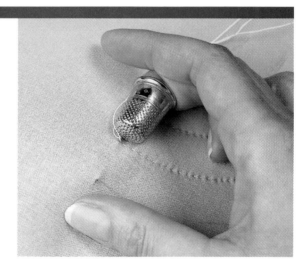

The simplest slide is when the distance you wish to cover is within a single needle length. As you complete the first line of quilting, insert the needle back into the same hole from which it emerged. **Run the needle *between* the top and the batting and bring it up at the start of the new area you wish to quilt.**

Tip

Don't pull too hard on the thread after sliding, or it may cause a pucker.

3

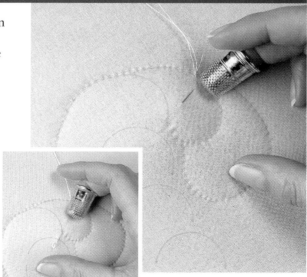

When the area to travel is greater than a needle length, you can still bridge the distance by sliding. Begin the slide as described in the previous step, but stop before pulling the needle completely free. Leave the needle's eye buried in the quilt. **Place your middle finger on the tip of the emerging needle and pivot, aiming the reversed needle in the desired direction. Push the tip of the needle until the eye emerges to complete the slide.** Be sure you are wearing a thimble!

To minimize stress on the "underground" thread, limit each long-distance slide to no more than a single pivot.

Tip

To help prevent misshapen lines and pulled stitches, avoid changing directions when you slide.

The Quilter's
Problem Solver

Troubleshooting Threads

Problem	Solution
Quilting threads tangle and twist.	❑ Let the threaded needle hang from the quilt; it will untwist automatically. ❑ Thread the needle with the end of the thread that comes off the spool, and knot the cut end. ❑ Run the thread through a cake of beeswax before you begin quilting. The beeswax not only helps prevent tangles, but strengthens the thread as well. ❑ Use a shorter length of thread. The ideal length is about 18 inches—the average distance from fingertip to elbow.
Waxed thread pulls batting through the quilt top.	Waxed thread, although less prone to tangling, is often sticky. Ironing the thread after waxing it takes away the stickiness. Thread several needles and wax the threads. Place the threads between sheets of paper towels or pieces of muslin and press them with a hot iron. This melts the wax and forces it into the thread fibers.

Skill Builder

Your hands perspire, the thimble slips, and you can't seem to grip the needle for those first few quilting stitches. Sound familiar?

❑ Take a tip from athletes and musicians. Keep a small project handy and spend a few moments *warming up* before tackling "the main event."

❑ Dust clammy hands with cornstarch or talcum powder to get a better grip.

❑ A tiny rubber finger cot secures a slippery thimble, while a rubber disk called a Needle Grabber grips an errant needle. Check your local quilt shop for both products.

Try This!

Use these tricks to get a reluctant thread through the needle.

Start off by cutting the quilting thread on an angle. If it won't go through after several tries, turn the needle around and try threading from the other side. Sometimes the production process makes one side of the eye smaller than the other. Lick the eye of the needle, rather than the cut end of the thread. Licking the needle wicks the thread through the eye more easily.

The Quilting *Stitch*

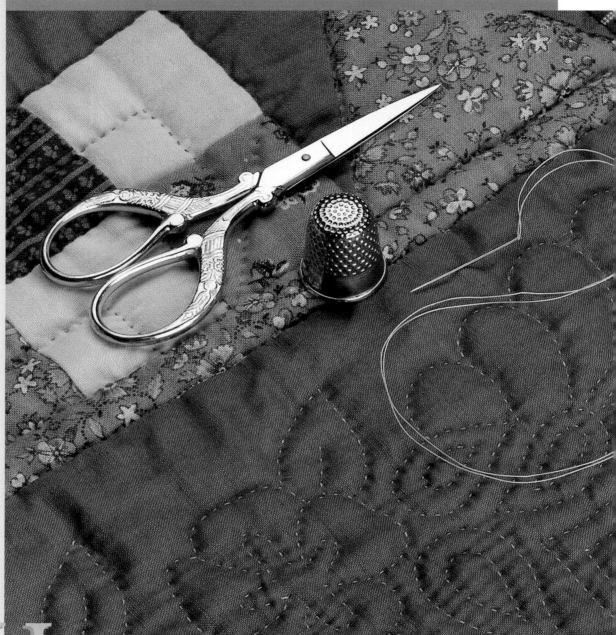

Hand quilting offers the best of both worlds. Once you have developed a comfortable rhythm, the quilting stitch requires minimal concentration. You can quilt while visiting or while watching TV with family and friends. On the other hand, many quilters describe the simple repetitive motion as meditative, making it the ideal activity for quiet contemplation. You can be as social—or as solitary—as you please!

Getting Ready

If you're new to hand quilting, it may take a little while to get used to the rhythm of the rocking stitch. Before you start stitching on your actual quilt, do some practice quilting on a smaller mock-up. Make an 18-inch quilt sandwich using the same fabric and batting that are in your quilt. Spend about 5 minutes doing some quilting on the smaller piece to get your fingers warmed up. Then when you move to the real quilt your muscles will already have practiced the rocking motion. Do this warmup before every quilting session.

What You'll Need

Basted quilt

Quilt hoop or frame

Betweens needles

Quilting thread

Thimble

Embroidery scissors or thread snips

Rocking Stitch

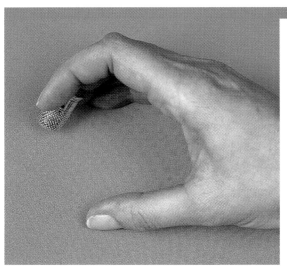

A good rocking stitch depends on holding the needle correctly. Rather than gripping it between your thumb and forefinger, as is usual for most hand sewing, you *guide* it instead, using your thumb and middle finger to do the work. **These fingers will curve into a "C" position, with the thimble on the middle finger.**

1

The hand you write with is the hand that should be wearing the thimble, doing the work on the top of the quilt.

2

The other hand stays beneath the quilt to feel the needle as it pierces all three layers and to guide it back up to the quilt top to complete each stitch. The index or middle finger commonly does this work.

Repeated pricks can cause sore fingertips. **Protect your under finger with a metal or leather thimble, or Aunt Becky's Finger Protector.** A coating of clear nail polish or Nu Skin (available at your local pharmacy) gives protection while still letting you feel the needle.

Tip

Strips of adhesive tape are an easy and inexpensive way to protect fingertips.

3

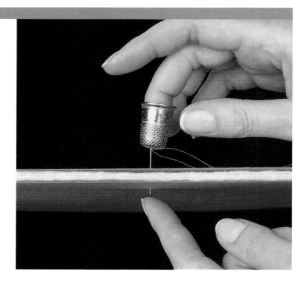

After burying the knot as described in "Starting, Stopping, and Sliding" on page 76, position the needle a single stitch length along the quilting line, reflecting the size you'd like subsequent stitches to be. **Place the needle so it is exactly perpendicular to the quilt top, balanced between the middle finger of the top hand and the index or middle finger of the guiding hand below.** No other fingers should be touching the needle.

Tip

The first stitch is the hardest one to make the same size as the rest. Concentrate on evenness when taking it.

4

Rest your thumb on the quilt top about ½ inch in front of the needle. *Gently* **push the needle straight down into the quilt to begin the first stitch.** You will feel the tip of the needle pierce the quilt back and touch the finger beneath the quilt.

5

Rocking the stitch means that both the hand on top and the one underneath must work together, in a simultaneous and fluid motion. Steps 5 and 6 need to happen at the same time.

As soon as you feel the needle come through to the underside of the quilt and make contact with the finger below, press up with that finger, just behind the tip of the needle. This provides the upward pressure required to return the needle to the top.

6

At the same time, press down firmly on the top of the quilt with your thumb, just past the "hump" formed by the finger below. **With the thimble-wearing middle finger, press the needle backward—like a lever—so that it is parallel to the quilt surface.** The opposing pressure of your thumb on top and your finger below will cause the point of the needle to pop through to the top of the quilt.

Do not pull the needle and thread completely through the layers to complete the stitch. **Instead, immediately begin the next stitch by returning the needle to a full vertical position, so that it is once again perpendicular to the quilt top.**

Tip

If you have trouble bringing the needle back to the vertical position, loosen the quilt in the hoop.

THE QUILTING STITCH

8

Repeat the procedure described in Steps 5 through 7 to load the second stitch onto the shaft of the needle. As soon as you have popped the needle back to the quilt top, begin a third and then a fourth stitch.

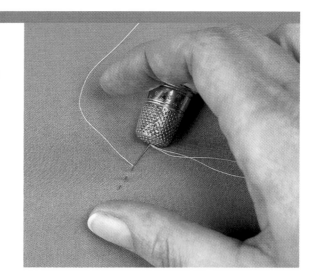

9

Tip

Resist the urge to constantly pick out quilting stitches! Too many stops and starts will prevent you from developing the rhythm essential to the rocking method.

Stack the needle with as many stitches as you can comfortably handle. Taking more than two stitches at a time keeps the stitches consistent in size and evenly spaced. Once you become comfortable with the rocking rhythm, you'll be able to stack four or five stitches on the needle without even thinking. Taking more than five stitches can make it difficult to pull the needle through the layers, and the needle is more prone to bend or break.

10

Tip

A deflated rubber balloon gives you a good grip to pull a loaded needle through stubborn quilt layers.

Use your top hand to grip and pull the loaded needle through the quilt layers. **Pull tightly enough so that the stitches snuggle on the surface of the quilt, but not so tight that they pucker.** Take a moment to admire your handiwork before repeating the entire process for the next sequence of stitches!

Just right

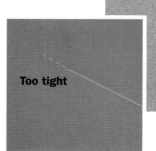

Too tight

Stab Stitch

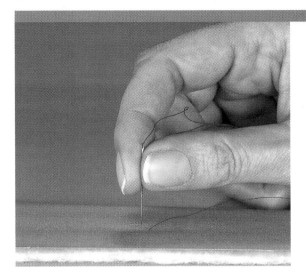

1

The stab quilting method tackles one stitch at a time. **Grasp the needle between the thumb and forefinger of your top hand.** Because you don't push the needle with your finger, you may not need a thimble to stab stitch.

Tip

If you have difficulty wearing a thimble, this may be the quilting stitch for you.

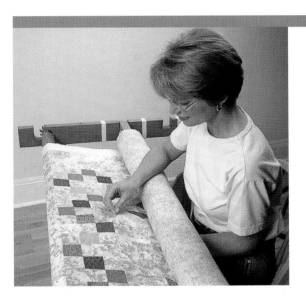

2

Although it *is* possible to use the stab stitch when quilting with a lap hoop, this method works best with a floor-standing hoop or frame. **Using a frame allows you to keep one hand on top, while the other is free to catch the needle coming through on the underside of the quilt.** Because the frame is stationary and self-supported, there is no need to juggle a hoop while trying to stitch.

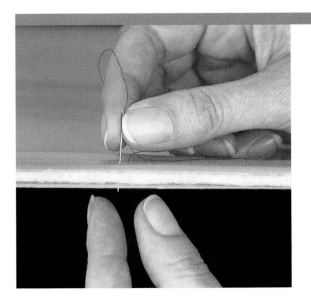

3

Begin with a buried knot as described in "Starting, Stopping, and Sliding" on page 76. Grasp the needle as shown in Step 1 and advance one stitch length. **Hold the needle perpendicular to the quilt surface, and insert it into the quilt top, pushing it through all three layers.**

THE QUILTING STITCH

4

Catch the needle between the thumb and forefinger of the underneath hand, and pull the threaded needle all the way through to complete the stitch. **Advance the needle one stitch length on the back of the quilt, and insert it so that it is perpendicular to the quilt back.** Push the needle straight up through all three layers.

5

Tip

If you have difficulty quilting through bulky seams, try stab stitching over the difficult part, then revert to the rocking method.

Pull the threaded needle all the way through the three layers to complete one stitch on the quilt back. Use enough tension so that the stitch lies snugly on the surface of the quilt, but does not cause the stitching to pucker. Repeat the process for subsequent stitches, finishing off with a buried knot.

6

Tip

To pull out a line of stitching, use a fine steel crochet hook. The tip of the hook tugs out the thread without snagging the fabric.

Keep individual stitches straight by focusing on the position of the needle as it passes from the top to the underside of the quilt and back again. **Crooked stitches are the result of angling the needle as it passes through the layers, rather than keeping it vertical.**

The stab stitch may seem a bit awkward at first, but you'll improve with patience and practice.

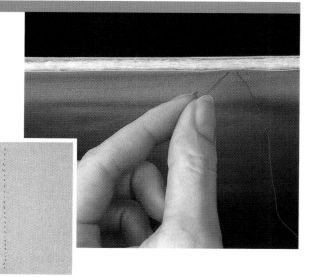

THE QUILTING STITCH

The Quilter's
Problem Solver

Broken Threads & Needles

Problem	Solution
Quilting thread frays or breaks.	Pull the thread, rather than the needle, when completing a needle load of stitches. Occasionally move the needle an inch or two along the length of quilting thread. This distributes the stress caused by the thread passing through the needle's eye. Another cause may be a burr in the eye of your needle. Try changing needles.
Needles constantly break.	Slightly loosen the tension in your quilting hoop or frame. There should be a slight give in the suspended quilt or you will have difficulty maneuvering the needle. You may be loading too many stitches on your needle at one time. Take fewer stitches in each load. Some needles are stronger than others, so experiment with different brands. Or, try the next larger size of your current favorite.

Skill Builder

If the very first stitch in your rocking sequence is larger than the others, correct the problem with these easy steps.

First, after you position your needle to make the first stitch, make a point to slide it a thread or two closer to where the thread exits the quilt. Then, be certain that you are inserting the needle exactly perpendicular to the quilt top. If the needle is angled rather than vertical, chances are the first stitch will be longer than you'd like.

Try This!

It can be very difficult to quilt through the bulky seams of patchwork quilts.

One solution is to quilt just the top and batting first, and then turn the quilt over and add quilting stitches just on the back layer. Sometimes you can avoid this problem by planning ahead. Minimize bulk by pressing particularly cumbersome seams open as you piece. Then plan quilting designs to cross as few seam lines as possible.

THE QUILTING STITCH

the stitch that is perfect for you!

*O*bserve any group of quiltmakers, and you'll quickly discover that the quilting stitch is as personal as a fingerprint. Yet despite the fact that each quilter places her own individual stamp on traditional techniques, there are certain basic standards that signal fine stitchery. Follow these few simple guidelines and you'll soon be making the stitch that is perfect . . . for you!

Getting Ready

The best way to analyze your quilting stitch is to do some stitching. Mark a simple motif on a piece of muslin or solid-color fabric and make a practice quilt sandwich. Include curves as well as straight lines in the quilting design so that you can check your skill in handling both. Use a contrasting thread, so your stitches will be easily visible on the front and back of your practice piece. Quilt on a portion of the design for a few minutes to warm up and develop your usual quilting rhythm. Circle this section so you know it's the warmup. Then finish stitching the motif. When you're done, use the information in this chapter to analyze your quilting, identifying both your strong points and those areas you might wish to improve.

What You'll Need

Quilt sandwich for practice

Quilt hoop or frame

Betweens needles

Quilting thread in a contrasting color

Thimble

Embroidery scissors or thread snips

Cake of beeswax (optional)

Stitch Length

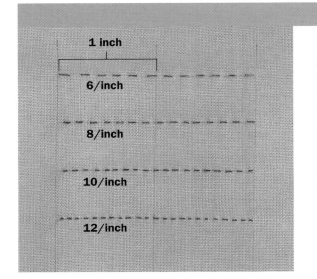

1 inch

6/inch

8/inch

10/inch

12/inch

While tiny stitches are not essential, it *is* important to the overall appearance and durability of your quilt that they are reasonably sized. If they are too large, they run the risk of being pulled loose or broken in the usual course of wear and care. **Anywhere from 6 to 12 stitches per inch is considered standard, counting only the stitches on top of the quilt.** In most cases, stitches will naturally become smaller with time, experience, and the development of a comfortable quilting rhythm.

The smaller the needle, the easier it is to make small stitches. Switch to the next smallest size as soon as you have mastered your current needle.

Stitch Size

Tip

The thickness of the batting may affect the size and consistency of your stitches. For smaller stitches, try a lower loft batting.

Although many quilters fret about the size of their stitches, most experts agree that it is equally—if not more—important that the stitches be *consistent*. **Ideally, stitches should be approximately the same size on both the front and back of the quilt, and the spaces between stitches should equal the stitch length.**

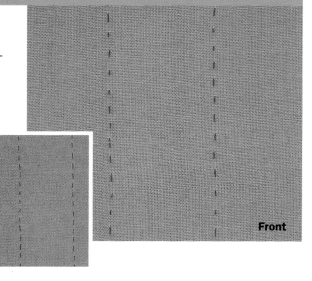

Back

Front

Straight Stitches

Your quilting should be straight. This applies not only to individual stitches, but to lines of quilting, too. The eye is easily distracted by a line that should be straight, but isn't. A wobbly line of quilting can make even the most precise piecing look distorted.

The rocking method (page 81) naturally lends itself to straight stitching. Because multiple stitches are loaded onto the needle, it is easier to achieve a smooth, consistent rhythm. The stab method (page 85), with its one-stitch-at-a-time approach, is a bit more difficult to control, but time and practice usually solve this problem.

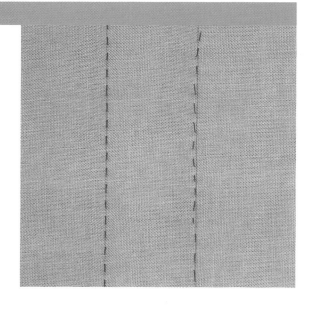

Curves

Tip

Stack at least two stitches on the needle before pulling the thread or you may have difficulty maintaining stitch consistency and tension.

Curved motifs should be smooth and flowing, with no rough or jagged edges. This can be tricky, particularly if you favor the rocking method. The challenge is magnified when the curves are tight or the circles small. Modify the number of stitches you load on the needle in each stitching sequence. Loading fewer stitches on the needle allows you to follow curved lines more easily.

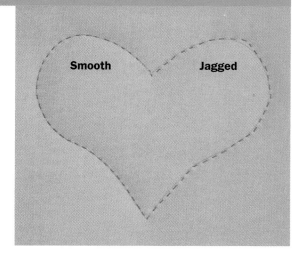

Smooth   **Jagged**

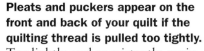

Pleats and puckers appear on the front and back of your quilt if the quilting thread is pulled too tightly. Tug lightly and consistently, maintaining an even tension on the thread. If the puckers persist, you may be stacking too many stitches on the needle. Take fewer stitches, or run the thread through beeswax to help it glide more easily through the layers (see page 79).

Skipped Stitches

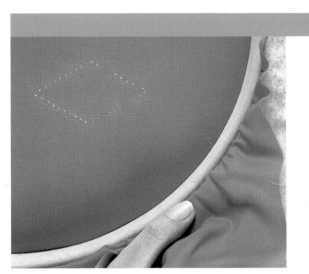

Every quilting stitch should be visible on the back, as well as on the front side of the quilt (see bottom half of the diamond). There should be no missed or skipped stitches (as shown on the top half of the diamond).

Skipped stitches are caused by angling the needle as you insert it into the quilt top. Remember to bring the needle to a full vertical position—perpendicular to the quilt top—before beginning *each* stitch, whether you are using the rocking or the stab-stitch method of quilting.

Stray Threads

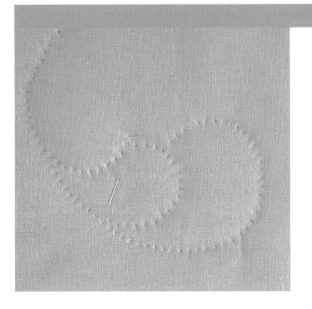

The start and finish of each stitching line should be invisible. Bury all knots, both the beginning and ending ones. If you use the knots shown in "Starting, Stopping, and Sliding" on page 74, there is no need to take a backstitch—a dead giveaway of a starting or stopping place.

Likewise, there should be no telltale sliding threads visible on either side of your quilt. Be sure you pierce only the top two layers when traveling from one line of stitching to another.

Tip

When you slide the thread from one spot to another, check the back for stray sliding threads before pulling the needle through.

ANATOMY OF A GOOD QUILTING STITCH

Quilting in a *Floor Frame*

The first time you sit down to quilt at a floor frame your hands may have no idea where to go. A quilt in a frame is in a fixed position, which means your stitching hand has to switch directions to follow the design (unlike a hoop where you can rotate the quilt into the most comfortable stitching position). But don't worry—there are lots of ways to make quilting in a frame feel like second nature.

Getting Ready

When you're quilting at a frame, the most comfortable directions are from right to left (for right-handed quilters), left to right (for lefties), and toward yourself. You can stitch the majority of designs in these directions. Everyone has a preferred way of working, but if you learn to expand your comfort zone to quilt in *every* direction, quilting in a floor frame will be even easier. There are times when the design will require you to stitch from front to back. Thumb quilting, although awkward at first, allows you to move in this direction. Learning to quilt with your other hand lets you stitch back and forth without having to stop, knot, and restart. To practice this new way of stitching, use a preprinted panel of fabric and make a commitment to stitch the entire piece with your other hand.

▶ *For information on installing a quilt in a floor frame, see "Installing a Quilt in a Frame" on page 68.*

What You'll Need

Quilt in a frame

Comfortable chair

Betweens needles

Quilting thread

Thimble

Embroidery scissors or thread snips

Protection for underneath finger (optional)

Thumb Quilting

1

Thumb quilting uses the same motion as "regular" quilting. The main difference is that you wear the thimble on your thumb. **Use the thimble to hold the needle vertically as it enters the fabric.** See "Choosing the Right Thimble" on page 14 for advice on selecting a comfortable thimble for your thumb.

2

When you feel the needle tip with your underneath finger, bring the back of the needle to a horizontal position and push it into the quilt. Push with the underneath finger to help guide the needle tip back up to the top of the quilt. At the same time, **press the fabric down in front of the tip of the needle with your index or middle finger.** This is how you form the first stitch.

3

Once the first stitch is on the needle, repeat the rocking process, moving the needle with the thimble from the vertical position to horizontal as you push the stitches onto the needle. **When you have two or three stitches on the needle, pull the thread through the fabric.**

Quilting in a Floor Frame

1

Begin quilting at the top of the quilt and stitch toward the bottom. This means that at first the bulk of the quilt is rolled up in front of you. By moving from top to bottom, you can quilt continuous designs without arbitrary stopping and starting places. This results in smoother quilting patterns, especially when you quilt border patterns or grids.

To choose your first line of quilting, start with the longest line. The easiest is a line that goes from right to left (opposite for lefties) or toward you. Thread the needle and quilt along the line until the thread runs out. Thread another needle and continue along the line as far as you can comfortably reach. When you've reached the end of the comfort zone, leave the threaded needle in the quilt. Pick up another needle and choose the next longest line. Quilt for as long as it's a comfortable reach, then leave the needle and thread in the fabric.

Tip

Thread a whole package of needles before you begin quilting, while your eyes are fresh.

Finish quilting all the parts of the design in the section you are working. When you have completed the section, move your chair, or roll the quilt if that is appropriate. **Pick up one of the needles you have left in the quilt and continue quilting along the line for as far as it is comfortable.** Continue until you have completed this section. Repeat for the remaining sections.

Tip

Save a needle left with a short thread after tying off for quilting shorter lines. Use a new pre-threaded needle for starting longer lines.

To quilt a circle or an oval, stitch it in two parts using a single thread. Thread the needle but don't tie a knot. Mentally divide the circle into segments equal to the divisions of a clock. **Bring the needle up at 1 o'clock and pull the thread halfway through; leave the other half dangling.** Lefties will find it easier to start at the 11 o'clock position. Quilt around the circle in one direction as far as you can, then tie off the thread. Rethread the needle with the dangling end and finish quilting the circle.

Tip

Use the same technique to quilt leaves. Start at one tip and quilt toward the other tip.

QUILTING IN A FLOOR FRAME

Larger stitches worked in heavier threads can add a wonderfully casual, country style to your quilt. This type of functional hand quilting has been used for years by quilters interested in getting a quilt together in a hurry and goes by the names utility, big stitch, and depression quilting. Coupled with the folk art look in piecing and appliqué, chunky stitches add the appropriate finishing touch. As an added bonus, not only will you finish more quilts in less time, taking bigger stitches is kinder to aching hands than taking tiny stitches with fine thread.

Getting Ready

The best candidates for country quilting are pieced or appliquéd country or primitive designs, scrap quilts, and projects that need the added punch of an overall quilting design and contrasting threads. On pieced quilts with many seams, the longer stitches make it easier to skip over the seams.

Select larger motifs and those with gentle curves, as well as grids and overall patterns. Accent appliqué designs by quilting ⅛ inch from the edge of the appliqué. Contrasting thread adds extra definition to the quilting design but makes any uneven stitches stand out. Matching thread disguises any stitch variations until you get the rhythm of making larger stitches.

The clamshell and the fan patterns are great choices for overall patterns. Stencils are readily available for both patterns, or you can easily draft them yourself using circles.

Clamshell

Fan

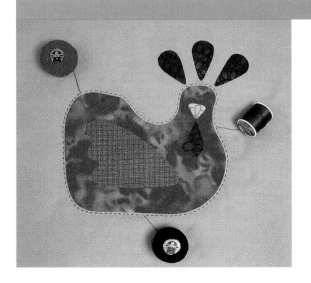

Threads

Pearl cotton, in size 8 or 12, is an excellent choice. Size 8 is equivalent to about three strands of embroidery floss; size 12 is a bit finer. Both are twisted, very strong, have a slight sheen, and come in many colors. **Topstitching thread is finer than either of the pearl cottons** but heavier than regular quilting thread, which allows it to create more design impact.

Tip

Embroidery floss is not a good choice for quilting because it is very soft and does not wear well.

COUNTRY-STYLE QUILTING

97

Stitching

COUNTRY-STYLE QUILTING

Tip

Size 7, 8, or 9 betweens needles will handle most threads. If these seem too small, try a small chenille needle.

1

Tie a quilter's knot (see "Starting, Stopping, and Sliding," page 75) with just a single twist of the thread around the needle; the knot will pop through the fabric easily but is still large enough to be secure.

Aim for 4 to 6 stitches to the inch. You decide which would be most appropriate based on the look of your quilt. If you are having trouble keeping your stitches even, take one stitch at a time until you establish a comfortable rhythm.

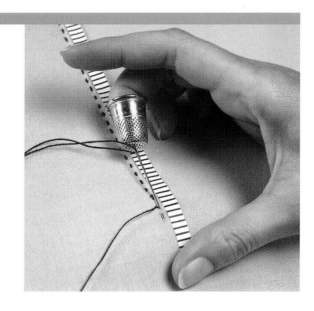

Tip

Mark your lines with Tiger Tape and use every other mark, rather than every one, to keep your stitches even.

2

Vary the stitch length and the spaces between for interesting effects. Consider stitches and spaces that are equal in length, larger stitches than spaces (Sashiko style), or smaller stitches and larger spaces.

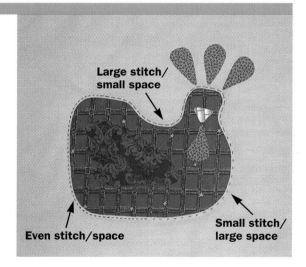

Large stitch/ small space

Even stitch/space

Small stitch/ large space

3

When you need to begin a new thread, keep the stitch-and-space sequence on the back the same. **Bring the new thread up in the same hole where the ending knot of the last strand went down. Go back down in the same hole and out the back of the quilt, then continue quilting.** The needle must go all the way through the back before you resume the quilting stitch. There won't be a stitch in that spot, but you'll be able to maintain the rhythm and keep the spacing the same.

To add some extra spice to the regular quilting stitch, weave a contrasting color thread in and out of the stitches. Knot the thread as usual and bring it up at the beginning of the line. Use thread or ⅛-inch-wide ribbon. Tie a knot at the end of the line and bury it in the batting.

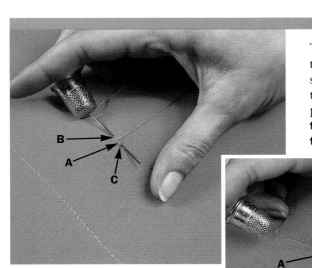

5

To create an even more definite line, try quilting with a backstitch. To start, bring the needle up at point A, then insert it about ⅛ inch back at point B. **Take a ¼-inch stitch, bringing the needle up about ⅛ inch in front of the thread at point C.**

To take the next stitch, insert the needle at point A, take a ¼-inch stitch, coming up about ⅛ inch in front of the thread. Continue to the end of the line.

Tip

Use a line of backstitching to emphasize a quilting design, such as a cable or a feather, or a particular shape in the pattern.

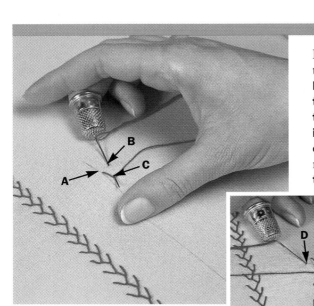

6

For even more interest and impact, try quilting with a feather stitch. **Bring the needle out at point A (on the quilting line), then move ¼ inch to the right and take a diagonal stitch, inserting the needle at B and coming out at C.** Loop the thread around the needle and pull it snug. **Move ¼ inch to the left and take a diagonal stitch, inserting the needle at point D, and coming up on the line at point E.** Always loop the thread under the needle as it comes back up on the quilting line.

Tip

Try quilting rope or cable designs with a featherstitch instead of the usual running stitch.

COUNTRY-STYLE QUILTING

Creative Twists on *Tying*

What do racehorses and crow's feet have to do with quilts? Plenty when they are descriptive names of attractive and easy stitches you can use to tie the three layers of a quilt together. While purists debate whether to call it a quilt if it's not quilted, you can be speedily tying your way through a mound of quilt tops. Besides the time-saving convenience, the decorative stitches shown here can add an appealing color and texture to the surface of your quilt.

Getting Ready

The easiest way to tie a quilt is to install it in a basting frame. Then you can just jump right in and start tying. But if you don't have a basting frame, either thread or pin baste the quilt before tying it.

Choose a batting that is needlepunched or made from bonded polyester. These battings will hold together without tearing or lumping even when you wash the quilt (as long as you do it gently). Decide where you want the ties and mark the spots if necessary. The easiest quilts to tie are those made with patterns of 3- to 4-inch squares; place the ties at the corners or in the centers of the squares. If the piecing does not provide a good pattern for tying, mark the quilt in a regular pattern of squares or diamonds.

For information on basting frames, see "Back-Saving Basting Frame" on page 60.

What You'll Need

Basted quilt or quilt in basting frame

Pearl cotton, baby-weight yarn, or ⅛" ribbon

Needles (style and size suitable for tying material used)

Fray Check

5⅛" doll needle

Racehorse Stitch

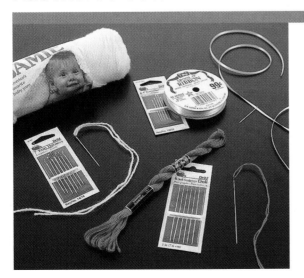

1

This continuous square-knot stitch moves quickly and can be done using pearl cotton, baby-weight yarn, or ⅛-inch ribbon. Pearl cotton and yarn make the longest wearing ties, while ribbon is more fragile. **Select a needle that puts a big enough hole in the fabric and batting to allow the thread, yarn, or ribbon through without pulling the batting to the surface.** Needle size is determined by the type of thread or yarn used. Cut a single strand 3 to 5 feet long and thread the needle with it.

2

Working from one end to the other, take a ¼-inch-long stitch at the first marked spot. Be sure that you pierce all three layers. **Leave a 2-inch tail of yarn, and tie a square knot.** Do not cut the yarn.

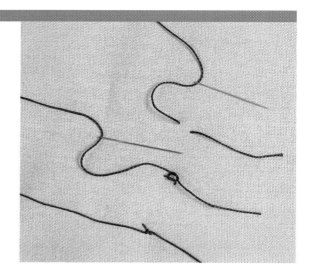

Tip

To make a square knot, remember "left over right, around and through, right over left, around and through."

3

Moving the needle about 3 to 4 inches to the left, or to the next marked spot on the quilt, take another ¼-inch stitch. **Loop the yarn in the needle over, then under the yarn strung between the first and second knots.** Pull the yarn tight. Knots should be spaced no farther apart than 3 to 4 inches.

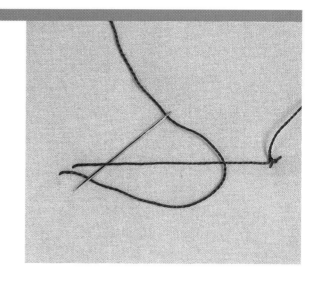

Tip

For variety, work rows of knots in a diagonal pattern.

4

Form a second loop by bringing the needle under the yarn strung between the first and second knot back over, then under the yarn from the second knot. This forms the square knot. Pull it tight to secure the knot.

Repeat the stitch at each of the next marked points, forming a row of square knots. **When the row is complete, cut the yarn between the stitches to the desired length.** Leave enough of a tail on the knots so they don't come untied.

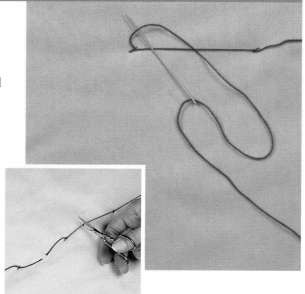

Tip

If you used ribbon for the ties, place a drop of Fray Check on the cut ends to prevent the ribbon from fraying.

Crow's Feet Stitch

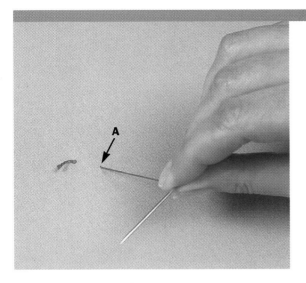

This stitch works best with pearl cotton and a 5⅛-inch doll needle. **Knot one end of the thread, insert the needle in the top layer and bring it out at the starting point (A). Tug gently to pop the knot through the top layer of fabric, burying it in the batting.**

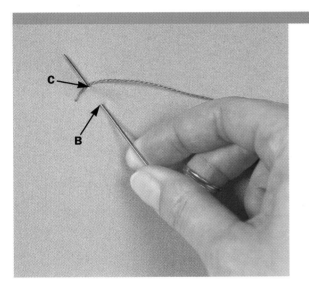

2

Looping the thread, insert the needle through all layers of the quilt at point B and out again at point C, making a ⅜- to 1-inch stitch. The size of the crow's feet is determined by the weight of the fabric. On lightweight fabric, make the stitches about ⅜ inch long; on heavier fabrics, they can be ½ to ⅝ inch long.

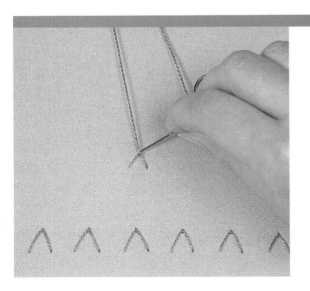

3

Make a small catch stitch over the thread, entering the top fabric and batting only. Slide the needle between fabric layers to begin the next stitch.

Work the stitches in straight vertical rows, or in diagonal rows, placing the stitches about 2 inches apart. (In our sample, we spaced ours closer together so you could see what kind of repeat pattern is created.) When you work in straight rows, the stitches on the back form a grid of single diagonal stitches.

Tip

Don't pull too tightly when you make the catch stitch; it will make a small pleat under the stitch and it won't lie flat.

CREATIVE TWISTS ON TYING

Easy
Grids

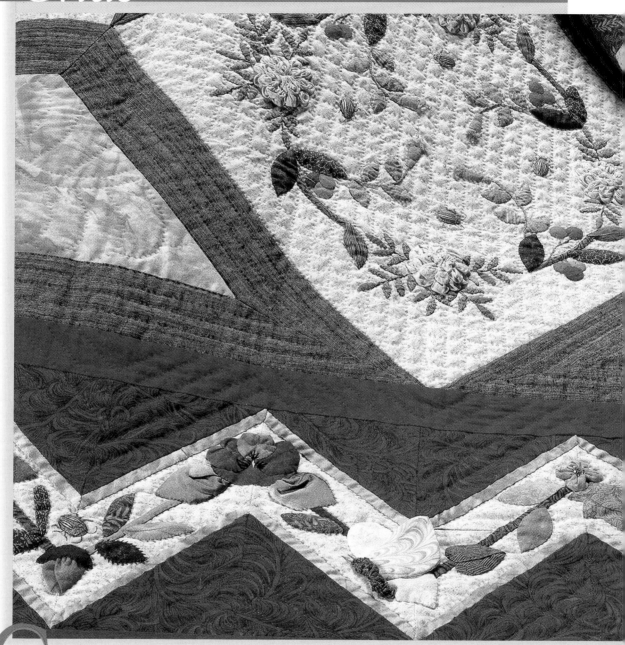

Grids, cross-hatching, and other straight-line patterns are traditional and classic designs that give an old-fashioned look to a quilt. They are ideal for adding quilting without introducing an additional design element, especially in a quilt where you want the piecing or appliqué to be the star. Sometimes less is more, and these designs are perfect for sweet, simple, antique-looking quilts.

Know Your Grids

What You'll Need

- **Unbasted quilt top**
- **Materials to make angle keeper:**
    - **8½" × 11" piece of paper**
    - **Cardboard or posterboard**
    - **See-through ruler with 45 and 60 degree angle lines**
    - **Pencil**
    - **Scissors or mat knife**
- **Marker of your choice**

Cross-hatching and grids work well in the background of an appliquéd block, as filler quilting in other designs such as feathered wreaths, and in borders or alternate blocks where a printed fabric would camouflage intricate quilting designs.

Keeping lines consistent and straight has been a stumbling block to many a quilter. Below are several ways to guarantee that your lines are arrow straight and don't wander across the quilt. Remember to keep the size of the grid in proportion to the quilt design. Consider the block size, the size of the patches, or the size of the appliqué motifs when determining the distance between the lines of quilting.

  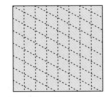 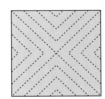

| Square Grid at 45° Angle | Diamond Grid at 60° Angle | Hanging Diamonds | X Grid |

Marking with an Angle Keeper

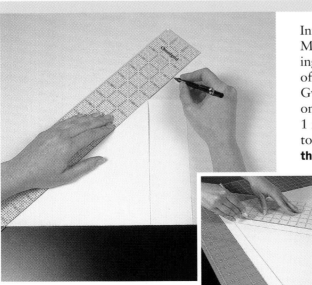

Internationally known quilter Gwen Marston came up with a simple but ingenious tool to solve the problem of wandering lines. She calls it Gwenny's Angle Keeper. To make one to mark 45 degree diagonals 1 inch apart, fold a piece of paper to create a 45 degree angle. **Transfer this 45 degree angle to a piece of cardboard or posterboard.**

Use a see-through ruler to draw another line parallel to the first 1 inch away. Draw a third line 1 inch above the bottom of the cardboard. **Cut out the shape and you're ready to mark.**

Tip

You can vary the angle and width of your angle keeper. Experiment to achieve the look you want.

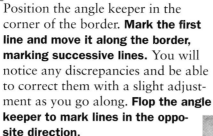

Position the angle keeper in the corner of the border. **Mark the first line and move it along the border, marking successive lines.** You will notice any discrepancies and be able to correct them with a slight adjustment as you go along. **Flop the angle keeper to mark lines in the opposite direction.**

Marking with a Ruler

1

To mark 60 degree diamonds, align the 60 degree angle on your ruler with a horizontal seam of the quilt. Position the ruler so that the first line will pass close to the center of the quilt and work out toward the sides. Mark the first line, move the ruler the desired distance, and mark the second line. Continue marking across the quilt. To mark grid lines in the opposite direction, move back to the center of the quilt and use the 60 degree line that slants in the opposite direction of the lines you just marked.

2

For hanging diamonds, align the 45 degree angle on your ruler with a horizontal seam of the quilt. Position the ruler so that the first line will pass as close to the center of the quilt as possible. Mark the first line, move the ruler the desired distance, and mark the second line. Continue marking across the quilt. **Then mark vertical lines across the quilt, at the same distance apart as the diagonal lines.**

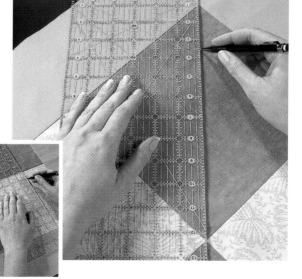

Double diagonals or "plaid" designs can be marked in a similar fashion. These directions are for marking a simple plaid. Beginning approximately in the center of the quilt, align the 45 degree angle on your ruler with a horizontal seam. Mark the first line, move the ruler ¼ inch away, and draw the second line. Move the ruler 1¼ inches, then ¼ inch, and so on. **Align the 45 degree angle of your ruler with a vertical seam and mark the lines going in the opposite direction.**

Tip

You can vary the distances and the sequence of doubling or even tripling the lines for endless variations.

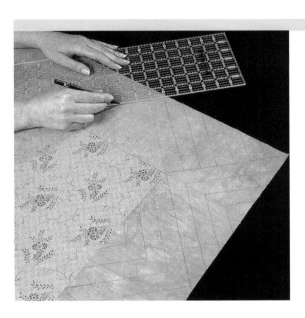

Grid variations make effective quilting designs in borders. These designs begin with diagonal lines marked in a V shape. Using a ruler, start at a corner and make a straight line from the inner corner to the outer corner. The easiest way to determine how many repeats you'll need is to make a folded paper border. (See "Designing Motifs to Fit" on page 42 for more information on fitting designs in borders.) Mark the divisions and draw a series of diagonal lines between them, alternating the direction of the lines. **Once you have the basic V shapes marked, you can add alternating parallel lines or smaller Vs or "tents."**

Tip

The June Tailor Grid Marker is a handy tool for marking grids of 45 and 60 degrees. See page 124 for a source.

How to Stitch

Do this

Avoid this

Grid quilting is usually done on the bias of the fabric. **When stitching in a block or on a background, quilt all the lines in one direction first. Then stitch all the lines that run in the opposite direction.** This helps avoid wrinkling and puckering. When quilting a grid in a border, stitch from the inner edge to the outer edge. Any fullness will ease out at the edges of the quilt. **When crossing another line of stitching, aim to have the stitch go underneath the previous line of stitching.** This will avoid having stitches overlap to form an X.

Tip

Don't plan to quilt an entire quilt with parallel straight lines or diagonals going in just one direction. It can cause distortion.

EASY GRIDS

Fearless *Feathers*

F luid and graceful, finely stitched feathers are guaranteed to make a quilter's heart
flutter. One of the most recognized and widely used designs, these graceful and elegant
plumes combine well with both pieced and appliquéd patterns. Considered a challenge
to draft, quiltmakers often resort to precut stencils or designs that may not be the best size or
configuration for the space. But once you understand the process, it is incredibly easy to
create your own feather designs.

Getting Ready

What You'll Need

- **Freezer paper or tracing paper**
- **Mechanical pencil with thin (.05) lead**
- **Ruler**
- **Quarter or dime or a plastic circle template**
- **Marker**
- **Template plastic (optional)**
- **Compass**
- **Colored markers or pencils**

Individual feathers can be long and skinny or short and fat. The most common proportion is a feather that is half to three-quarters as wide as it is high. For example, a 1-inch-tall feather looks best when it is ½ to ¾ inch wide.

Determine the finished size shape or area you want to fill with quilted feathers. Draw this shape on the dull side of freezer paper or on tracing paper. Decide how tall and wide you want your feathers to be. Make sure you leave some breathing room (at least ¼ to ½ inch) around the edges.

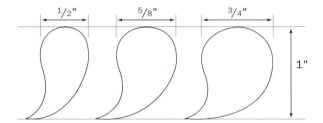

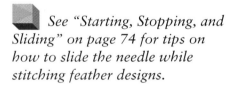 *See "Starting, Stopping, and Sliding" on page 74 for tips on how to slide the needle while stitching feather designs.*

Straight Feathers

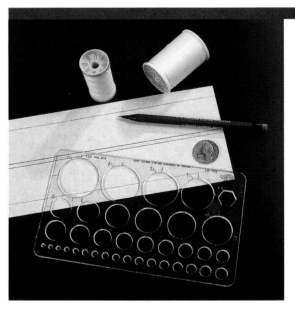

1

Draw the vein of the feather through the center of the paper. For all but very small motifs, a double line gives more definition to the design. Add guidelines on either side of the center vein equal to the height of the feather. The distance between the two guidelines will be the total width of the feathered motif.

Determine the width for the individual feathers, referring to the common proportions in "Getting Ready" above. **Find a circle the same size of the width of the feather.** Try a coin or the top of a spool of thread, or purchase a plastic stencil with many different sizes of circles.

Tip

The diameter of a quarter is 1"; a dime is ¾" wide.

FEARLESS FEATHERS

2

Beginning at one end, place the
circle template so the upper edge
just touches the inside of the top
guideline; **trace an arc around
the top half of the circle. Slide
the circle along the line and draw
another arc.** The circles should
connect at the sides and their
tops should just touch the
guideline. **Keep drawing arcs to the
end of the line, then do the same
along the bottom guideline.** The arcs
should be directly opposite each other.

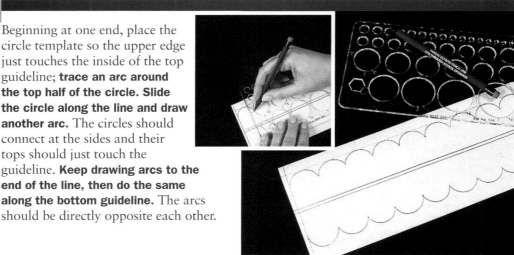

3

Draw dotted guidelines perpendicular
to the center vein at the points where
the arcs touch. These will determine
the spot where each feather tail ends.
Draw the tails of the feathers, connecting the edge of one arc with the
guideline that follows it. **Curve
the line gently so it meets the
center vein at the intersection
with the guideline.** Feathers
look best when the tails on
both sides don't match exactly
along the center vein. **Stagger
the tails on the second side so
they end about ⅛ inch ahead
of the tails on the first side.**

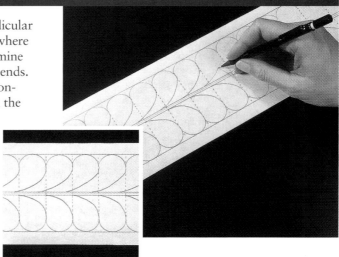

4

To make the ends of the straight
feather look identical, reverse the direction of the feathers in the center.
Find and mark the center point on
the paper. Add upper and lower
guidelines. Draw the arcs, beginning
at the center rather than at one end.
Draw the perpendicular guidelines,
then add the feather tails, beginning
in the center and working out to
the ends. **Curve the tails on each
side toward the center. Hearts
are formed along the centerline
where the tails of the reversed
feathers meet.**

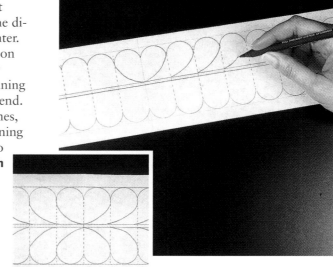

Straight feather designs need a graceful finishing touch at each end. **Complete the arcs at one end by extending their lines to form the tip of a heart.** At the other end, complete the arcs so their lines join to make the curved lobes of a heart. **Add a single feather to the center of the heart. For an extra flourish, add a smaller feather on each side of the single feather.**

Go over the finished feather with a marker to create a tracing guide to use with a light box (see "Marking Made Easy" on page 48). Or, use it to cut your own stencil (see "Designing Motifs to Fit" on page 42).

Feather Wreaths

1

Use a compass to draw a circle for the center vein; draw inner and outer guideline circles an equal distance from the center circle. These guidelines mark the height of the feathers. **Fold the circle in half, then quarters, then eighths.** Use these marks to space the outer edges of the feathers equally around the design. Draw the arcs as you did for the straight feather, fitting an equal number of arcs between each fold on the outer ring. Draw arcs on the inner ring, adjusting the width to fit the space if necessary.

The arcs should be the same size on the inner and outer circles, allowing for a slight adjustment for fit.

2

Mark the center ring opposite the intersection of each arc in the outer ring (shown in black in the photo). Draw the tails of the outer ring of feathers, making sure they curve smoothly toward the center. **Using a different colored marker (red is used here), mark the center ring opposite the intersection of each arc in the inner ring.** Draw in these tails. They will not meet the vein in equal increments as they do on a straight line.

F E A R L E S S   F E A T H E R S

Hand
Trapunto

L ong associated with heirloom quilts, trapunto is still the hallmark of exquisite hand quilting. The raised quilting design contrasts with the texture and shadows of the rest of the stitching to add dimension and accentuate special motifs. Trapunto takes a little more work than regular hand quilting, but it's not difficult to do and doesn't require a lot of special supplies.

Getting Ready

Quilters borrowed the word *trapunto* from Italian and apply this single term to two different quilting techniques: stuffed and corded trapunto. Stuffed trapunto calls for quilting the outline of a shape, then stuffing it with batting. In corded trapunto, parallel lines are quilted first, then stuffed with yarn. Before you start, decide which method you will be doing. The trapunto motif can help you determine the best technique. Large or elaborate motifs are better stuffed with batting; small details or straight or curved linear designs can be done easily with yarn.

When you select your motif for trapunto, be sure to choose a design that has enclosed parts or sections, otherwise the lines of quilting won't contain the stuffing. The teardrop shapes in a feathered wreath or vine are perfect for stuffing, for instance.

What You'll Need

- **Quilt top, batting, and backing**
- **Marking tool**
- **Quilting thread and needles**
- **For stuffed trapunto:**
  - **Batiste or other thin fabric**
  - **Basting thread and needle**
  - **Embroidery scissors**
  - **Fiberfill or batting**
  - **Orange stick, awl, or blunt needle**
- **For corded trapunto:**
  - **Acrylic knitting yarn**
  - **Blunt yarn needle or trapunto needle**

Stuffed Trapunto

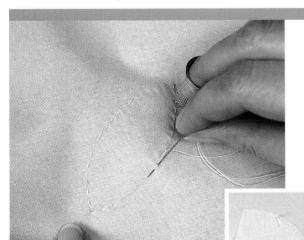

1

To stuff motifs with batting, mark the design on the quilt top. Lay a piece of batiste or other lightweight fabric underneath the area to be stuffed (on the wrong side), and baste in place. **From the right side, baste all lines that will be quilted just inside the marked line with medium-length stitches.** Use white thread for basting, as colored thread may leave dots of dye in the fabric when it is removed. **Trim away the excess batiste beyond the basted area.**

Tip

Use water-soluble thread for basting the batiste in place. Wash or spritz with water to remove it.

HAND TRAPUNTO

Tip

Be careful! Don't clip the quilt top when making slits or punch through it with the stuffing tool.

Cut a small slit in the batiste within the basted design, and push fiberfill or a small scrap of batting into the design with an orange stick or other blunt tool. You may need to make a slit in each area of the design to fill it without stretching the basting.

Stuff a small amount of filling at a time to avoid forming lumps or overstuffing. The area should be gently raised, without creating a hard lump on the surface of the quilt. **Hold the stuffing in place by sewing closed the slits in the lining.**

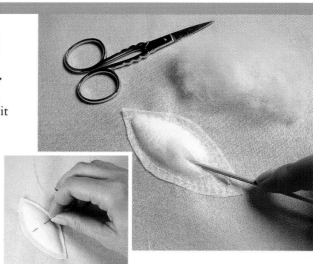

Tip

Keep the quilt fairly taut in the frame or hoop so the trapunto does not distort the background while it is being quilted.

When the trapunto is finished, layer and baste the quilt with low-loft batting and permanent backing. **Quilt just beyond the basting lines of the trapunto, then remove the larger basting threads.**

To create contrast between the trapunto and regular quilting, the background quilting must be close enough so that the trapunto stands out in relief. Add echo or stipple quilting around trapunto, or surround the other quilting motifs with cross-hatching.

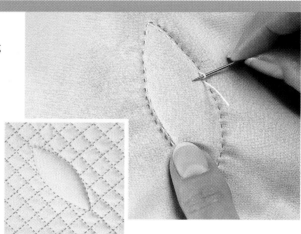

Corded Trapunto

Following your chosen quilting design, stitch parallel lines of quilting. These create the channel that will be filled with yarn. **The width of the cording channel depends primarily on the proportion of the design.** It also depends on the type of yarn being used. Thicker yarn won't fit easily in a very narrow channel. With narrower knitting yarn, you may need to use more than one layer of yarn to fill a channel. A good rule of thumb is to start with a ¼-inch-wide channel and adjust from there. The channel should be no wider than ⅜ inch.

114

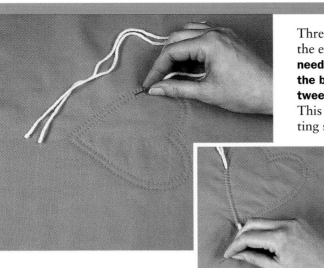

Thread a yarn or trapunto needle so the ends of the yarn match. **Insert the needle into the quilted channel from the back of the quilt, keeping it between the batting and the backing.** This way, the yarn will raise the batting smoothly and evenly without showing through the quilt top. If the channel is longer than the needle, slide the needle along inside the channel to the end. **Bring the needle out of the channel, and pull the yarn so it disappears into the channel.** Clip the yarn flush with the fabric where the needle exited.

Tip

Don't pull too tightly when filling a curved channel. If the yarn draws up or puckers the design, pull it out and start over.

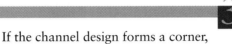

If the channel design forms a corner, don't try to turn it with the needle or you'll pull the corner out of alignment. Stuff one side of the design at a time, exiting at each corner. **To begin the next side, reinsert the needle in the same hole from which it exited the previous channel.** You don't even have to cut the yarn. If it's long enough, you can simply reinsert the already-threaded needle. Sticking the trapunto needle into the backing fabric will push the fibers apart. **To close the "hole," use a blunt needle to push the threads of the backing fabric into place.**

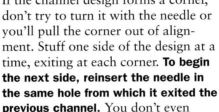

Tip

Use yarn that matches the backing fabric and any fibers that linger won't be noticed. However, be sure colored yarn doesn't show through the top.

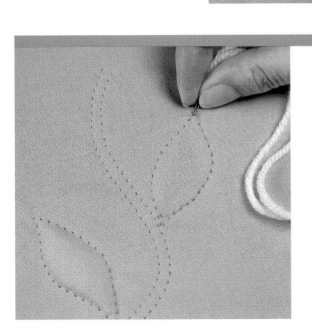

Small motifs can be stuffed with yarn in the same way channels are corded. You'll need to add two or more rows of yarn until the area is stuffed. For rounded shapes, such as a feather or leaf motif, stuff the outer edges (against the quilting stitches) first. **Since the needle is straight and motifs are usually curved, once the first yarn is inserted in the shape, reinsert the tip of the needle in the hole and use it to push the yarn snugly against the side of the shape.** Continue filling from outer edges toward the center, clipping the yarn after each row is added.

Tip

Use high-loft yarn for filling shapes, since it fills well without leaving any lumps.

HAND TRAPUNTO

Sensational
Stipple Quilting

Hand stipple-quilted projects practically guarantee heirloom status. But it's not just the abundant stitching that creates the look we love. It's the wrinkles and the creases that are formed in the small areas between the stitches that provide texture, and texture is what stippling is really about. Stipple quilting recesses the fabric around quilted, appliquéd, or trapuntoed motifs, providing the additional benefit of highlighting the designs. Yes, it's more time-consuming, but if results are what you're after rather than finishing first, this background-quilting technique is a winner.

Getting Ready

Simply defined, stippling refers to the quilting technique of sewing lines of stitching close together, approximately ¹⁄₁₆ to ⅛ inch apart. The most recognized stipple pattern (a nonpattern, really) is a meandering line that curves in and out, creating shapes that look like pieces from a jigsaw puzzle. To be authentic, it should be a continuous line, but since starting and stopping can be accomplished invisibly when you're hand quilting, no one will ever know.

Other well-known quilting patterns like checkerboard, diamond, and chevron can be adapted for stippling quilt backgrounds. You'll need to mark them ¹⁄₁₆ to ⅛ inch apart. Echo quilting, or repeating the shape of a design with closely stitched concentric lines of quilting, is a good alternative because it doesn't require any marking.

What You'll Need

Quilt top, batting, and backing

Quilting thread (color to match fabric)

Paper and pencil

Removable marking pen or pencil (optional)

Quilt hoop or frame

Betweens needles

Thimble

Embroidery scissors

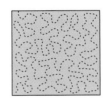

Checkerboard   Diamond   Chevron   Echo   Meander

Meander Stipple Quilting

1

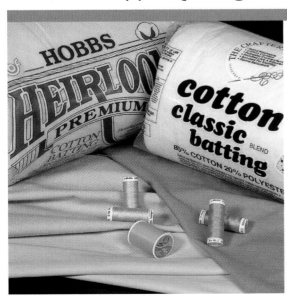

Stippling is most effective when solid fabric and matching thread are used. The pattern in a print fabric camouflages the stitches and high contrasting thread overpowers the subtle designs. The texture you're spending all that time to create will not be as evident. **For the best texture and easiest needling, use cotton/polyester blend batting.** The polyester makes the batt spring back a little bit, accentuating the stitches and creating the shadows that make the textured look. Thick batts make it difficult to create tiny stitches. Thin batts, particularly all cotton ones, don't give any depth to the stitching, so the shadowing and texture are lost.

2

Loosen up by drawing freehand some practice meandering lines. **Take a sheet of paper and mark on it a portion of your quilt design where you want to add stippling.** Make several photocopies of this practice sheet so you have plenty of extras. **With a pencil, begin drawing a meandering line of jigsaw-puzzle shapes.** Keep the curves uniform in size and vary the direction of the line. Try to maintain consistent spacing of 1/16 to 1/8 inch between the quilting lines.

3

Once you're comfortable with creating the pattern with paper and pencil, it's time to graduate to needle and thread. Quilting these squiggly lines freehand, without marking, saves time and the frustration of having to stitch precisely on the line. **But until your confidence and experience grow, you can draw a path to follow with your favorite removable marking tool.** Trace from your practice sheets if there's a meander that you like.

4

Tip

Secure your quilt in a hoop or frame to help prevent distortion when quilting so densely.

Begin stitching in a corner or a tight space and work out to open spaces. Do *not* stitch parallel to the outline of the motif (shown to the lower right of the leaf). Instead, keep the meandering lines of stitches perpendicular to help distinguish the stippling from the motif (see the stippling to the left of the leaf).

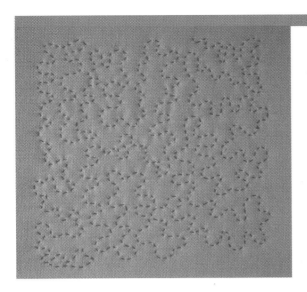

Another key to successful meander stippling is changing direction often. Work the stitching pattern around itself rather than in rows. Always keep those jigsaw-puzzle pieces in mind as you stitch. Maintain the "innie" and "outie" shapes.

Shorten your sewing time by stitching jigsaw shapes ¼" apart instead of using the ⅟₁₆ to ⅛" spacing.

6

If you quilt yourself into a corner, slide the needle to another area and resume stitching. (See "Starting, Stopping, and Sliding" on page 78 for pointers on how to slide.) Or, you can end that thread with a knot and start in the new area with a new knot. Stopping to slide or knot are unavoidable when you're working around intricate motifs.

Meander stippling, with all its twists and curves, doesn't allow you to gather four or five stitches on the needle at a time. **To obtain gentle curves rather than harsh, pointy corners, take two stitches, angling them slightly, and pull them through.** Very tight curves may require only one stitch at a time.

Hand Quilting *Glossary*

Appliqué. Sewing smaller pieces of fabric to a larger background, usually to form a realistic or pictorial pattern.

Background quilting. Repetitive motifs, such as grids, clamshells, or checkerboards, used in open areas of a quilt; they enable other designs to come forward to catch the viewer's eye.

Backing. The fabric that is used for the "wrong" side of a quilt to hold the batting layer in place. Backings can be made from one piece of fabric or several lengths pieced together to reach the appropriate size. Backings can also be pieced for a decorative look. Sometimes referred to as "lining."

Basting. The process of temporarily securing the three layers of a quilt together in preparation for quilting. Can be done using needle and thread, pins, or basting gun.

Basting gun. A timesaving device that injects plastic tacks through all layers of a quilt to secure them for quilting.

Batting. The invisible layer in a quilt. Usually made of cotton, polyester, wool, or two blended fibers, batting is available in a variety of thicknesses. The fiber content of a batt dictates how close or far apart the quilt can be quilted to retain its shape, as well as how the finished quilt needs to be laundered.

Bearding. A fuzzy or "bearded" appearance that occurs when batting fibers work their way through the quilt top or backing. This condition happens primarily with polyester battings.

Beeswax. A waxy substance rubbed on thread to help stiffen and strengthen it, and reduce tangles.

Betweens. Short, sturdy needles used for hand quilting. Betweens come in sizes ranging from 5 to 12. The rule of thumb is the bigger the number, the shorter the needle.

Channel stencil. A quilting template with narrow slots cut along the design. A marker inserted and slid along the slots transfers the template design to the quilt top.

Corded trapunto. A pattern of closely spaced parallel lines that are quilted, then stuffed with yarn to add depth to the design.

Cording. The string or yarn used to stuff lines of trapunto designs. Different diameters of cording can be used to create different looks. Cording options include pearl cotton, yarn, and cotton cording.

Country quilting. Functional hand quilting, usually worked with a heavy thread like pearl cotton and larger stitches to produce a folk art, country appearance.

Cross-hatching. A grid of parallel quilting lines that form diamonds or squares on the background of a block or a whole quilt. Cross-hatching may be done diagonally or on the straight of grain.

D

Darning needles. Long, heavier needles with blunt points occasionally used in place of a hera to mark small, finely detailed areas of a quilt top.

D-hoop. A specialty hoop, shaped like the letter D. When attached to the outer edge of a quilt, it provides even tension for better quilting.

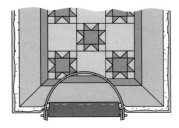

Doll needles. Very long (up to about 5 inches long), fine but strong needles occasionally used in place of a hera to mark smaller, more detailed areas of a quilt top.

Drape. The amount of softness versus stiffness in a batt, which affects the appearance of a finished quilt. Quilts made with a soft, thin batt drape more easily on a bed than those made with stiff, thick batts.

E

Echo quilting. Concentric lines of quilting that produce repeating, or echoed, shapes. Echo quilting is most often used around appliqué shapes and quilted motifs. Rows of echo quilting can be spaced equally or by varying amounts.

H

Hera. A traditional Japanese marking tool that leaves a sharp crease where it is pulled across fabric. The crease is used to indicate stitching or quilting lines.

L

Light box. A glass- or Plexiglas-topped box containing a bright light that makes tracing quilting pattens a breeze. Commercially made light boxes are available from quilt shops or art supply stores. You can make a temporary version by placing a light beneath any glass or Plexiglas table.

Loft. The term used to describe the thickness of batting. Thicker, high-loft batts result in puffier quilts; thinner, low-loft ones yield flatter quilts.

M

Marking. The process of transferring quilting designs onto the quilt top. Designs can be marked through a cut stencil with a marking pencil or traced from a printed pattern placed underneath the quilt top.

Meander quilting. Random quilting lines that resemble pieces of a jigsaw puzzle, and that usually don't cross over one another. When very closely spaced, the lines are called stipple quilting; mean-

dering lines are more widely spaced.

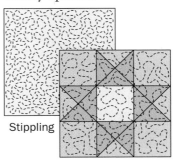

Stippling

Meandering

Milliner's needles. Long, fine, sharp needles often used for basting and tying.

N

Needlepunching. A finishing technique used by manufacturers in which batting fibers are punched with special needles to bind them together. Needlepunched battings resist bearding. Both cotton and polyester battings can be needlepunched.

Needle threader. A tool with a fine wire loop that is inserted through the eye of a needle to grasp thread and draw it through the eye.

O

Outline quilting. Outlining a shape with a line of quilting stitches, often placed ¼ inch from the seam.

Outline stencil. A pattern made by cutting away a shape from template material, then tracing around the inside of the resulting "window."

HAND QUILTING GLOSSARY

Overall quilting. Quilting that covers the entire surface of the quilt with one repetitive design. Clamshell and fan designs are examples of commonly used overall quilting designs.

P

Patchwork. Small pieces of fabric sewn together to form a larger unit, quilt block, or quilt top.

Pearl cotton. A silky-looking, heavy cotton thread used for folk art or country quilting, embroidery, and tying.

Pouncing. A marking technique in which a chalk-filled bag or other container is moved up and down on top of a stencil to transfer lines to fabric placed beneath it.

Q

Quilting frame. Also called a floor frame. A large, freestanding frame that secures the quilt top, batting, and backing layers together so they can be quilted. Stretcher-style frames make the entire quilt surface available for quilting at the same time. With a roller-style frame, the quilt layers are rolled on long poles and only a portion of the quilt is available to stitch on at a time.

Three-Roller Frame

Quilting hoop. A round or oval two-part "frame" that holds the layers of a quilt sandwich together and secure for hand stitching. A screw and bolt allow for tightening or loosening tension. The hoop is repositioned as you work.

Quilting in the ditch. Placing quilting stitches a needle's width away from a seam line to define a design in a quilt.

Quilting thread. Specialized thread that is slightly heavier than regular sewing thread. It comes waxed to pull more smoothly through the fabric layers and to add strength and prevent tangling.

Quilt sandwich. Term commonly used to describe the three layers of a quilt: the top, the batting, and the backing.

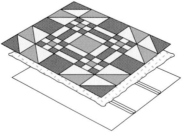

R

Rail. The part of a quilt frame around which the quilt top, batting, and backing are rolled.

Repeat. The unit in a quilting design that is duplicated, side by side, with other identical units to create the design.

Rocking stitch. The dual-action motion in hand quilting, where the hand on top and the hand un-

derneath work together to move the needle in a fluid, back-and-forth rhythm between vertical and horizontal positions. This motion allows you to load multiple stitches onto the needle before pulling it through the fabric.

S

Scrim. A lightweight, non-woven material that is added to batting to enhance stability.

Selvage. Tightly woven, finished edges that run lengthwise along the fabric. They should be trimmed away and not used.

Sliding. Moving from the end of one quilting line to the beginning of the next without clipping and re-knotting the thread. Also referred to as traveling.

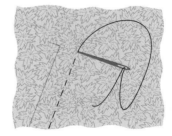

Stab stitching. Taking only one quilting stitch at a time with separate motions for pushing the needle to the underside of the quilt and bringing it back to the top again.

Stipple quilting. Very closely spaced, random lines that resemble pieces of a jigsaw puzzle; generally used to fill in small areas or flatten portions of a quilt in order to emphasize nearby raised motifs.

Stuffed trapunto. Quilted motifs that are raised by stuffing them from behind with batting.

Tailor's thimble. An open-ended metal thimble with deep dimples around the sides that is worn on the thumb when thumb quilting.

Template. An exact copy of a pattern piece constructed from a sturdy material like template plastic so that it can be traced around many times onto fabric without distorting its shape. Commonly used in piecing, templates are also used in quilting, where a simple quilting motif is cut from plastic, then traced around onto the quilt top.

Thimble. A sturdy device that protects a finger from needle pricks during hand sewing. When quilting, it is used to steady and guide the needle as it moves downward through the quilt sandwich.

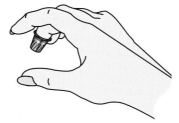

Thumb quilting. A technique in which the thumb holds the needle in a vertical position as it enters the top of a quilt sandwich.

Tracing guide. A working copy of a quilting pattern that is used to help transfer a motif to fabric.

Tracing paper. Lightweight see-through paper that is available in art supply or department stores. It comes in sheets or on a roll. When tracing paper is placed over a design in a book, the lines are easily visible and can be copied to the paper, then transferred to fabric or template material.

Tying. Placing single, individually tied stitches at intervals across the surface of a quilt. A variety of different stitches and knots can be used to create interesting effects.

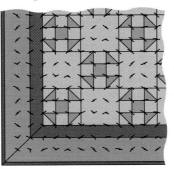

Specific Products & Supplies

Most of the equipment shown in the photographs is available at your local sewing or quilt shop or in sewing or quilting catalogs. Check these sources for specific products or patterns.

Aunt Becky's Finger Protector—Jannilou Creations, 1243 Main, PO Box 333, Philomath, OR 97370 - (541) 929-3795

Bird Parade appliqué pattern—Red Wagon Designs, 456 E. Kansas Ave., Liberty, MO 64068 - (816) 792-1540

Fern stencil—Mary Stori, 6 Coldren Dr., Prospect Heights, IL 60070

Floral appliqué patterns—Heirloom Stitches by Pat Andreatta - (800) 261-4218

Grace Quilting Frames—PO Box 27823, Salt Lake City, UT 84127 - (800) 264-0644

June Tailor Grid Marker—Keepsake Quilting

Mountain Mist Quilting Frame Blueprint—The Stearns Technical Textiles Company, Consumer Products Division, 100 Williams St., Cincinnati, OH 45215 - (800) 345-7150

Ott-Lite—Little Foot, Ltd., 605 Bledsoe NW, Albuquerque, NM 87107 - (505) 345-7647

Paddle Thimble—House of Quilting, Rt. 3, Box 433, Fayetteville, NC 28306 - (910) 868-3842

Roxanne's Quilting Thimbles and Needles—Roxanne International, 3009 Peachwillow La., Walnut Creek, CA 94598 - (800) 993-4445

Specialty threads—Web of Thread, 1410 Broadway, Paducah, KY 42001 - (502) 575-9700

General Quilt Supplies

Clotilde, Inc.
B3000
Louisiana, MO 63353-3000
(800) 772-2891
Fax: (800) 863-3191

Connecting Threads
PO Box 8940
Vancouver, WA 98668-8940
(800) 574-6454

Keepsake Quilting
Rt. 25B, PO Box 1618
Centre Harbor, NH 03226
(800) 865-9458

Nancy's Notions
333 Beichl Ave.
PO Box 683
Beaver Dam, WI 53916-0683
(800) 833-0690

The Quilt Farm
PO Box 7877
Saint Paul, MN 55107
(800) 435-6201
Fax: (612) 293-0204

Quilts and Other Comforts
(800) 881-6624
Fax: (888) 886-7196

Jane Hall and **Dixie Haywood** are award-winning quiltmakers who are known for adapting traditional designs using contemporary techniques and innovative approaches. Their quilts have been exhibited throughout the country and are in private and public collections. Both have been teaching and judging quiltmaking for more than 20 years and have a strong commitment to provide students with well-grounded and creative information so they can make their own unique quilts. They have coauthored *Perfect Pineapples, Precision Pieced Quilts Using the Foundation Method,* and *Firm Foundations.* Jane is a certified appraiser for old and new quilts. Dixie is the author of *Contemporary Crazy Quilt Project Book* and *Crazy Quilting with a Difference,* and her articles appear regularly in leading quilt periodicals. Longtime friends, Jane lives in Raleigh, North Carolina, with her husband, Bob; Dixie lives in Pensacola, Florida, with *her* husband, Bob. They rely heavily on the telephone, fax, and airlines to function as a team.

Cyndi Hershey has been quilting since 1978 and began teaching quilting in the early 1980s. Her background is in interior design and textiles. The colors, patterns, and textures of fabric are still the things that interest her the most. Being able to combine so many different fabrics in one project is the primary reason that she loves quilting. She and her husband, Jim, bought the Country Quilt Shop in Montgomeryville, Pennsylvania, in 1988. Her favorite part of owning the shop is that it allows her to teach as often as possible, helping other quilters learn and grow.

Carol Johnson has a graphics art and journalism degree from Utah State University. She belongs to local, state, and national quilt guilds, has taught quilting throughout Utah, and has written for books and quilting magazines. Her quilts have been exhibited in local, state, and national contests. She specializes in making and teaching how to make tied coverlets and uneven, curved, pieced, and quilted scenes from nature. She and her husband live in Nibley, Utah, and are the parents of six children.

Sue Linker has been quilting for 22 years and teaching since 1978. She is the author of *Sunbonnet Sue All through the Year.* Her classes in appliqué techniques and fine hand quilting are popular throughout the Pacific Northwest and fill quickly. She is also known for her eclectic fabric collection. Several years ago she began experimenting with country quilting and with using embroidery stitches for quilting. Sue lives in Sumner, Washington, with her husband, Jim, and not too far away from her 10 grandchildren.

Gwen Marston is a professional quiltmaker, author, and teacher who has written 12 books and produced a series of videos on quiltmaking. She has taught quilting across the United States and in Japan and has been a regular columnist for *Lady's Circle Patchwork Quilts* magazine for 11 years. Her recent book, *Quilting with Style: Principles for Great Pattern Design,* gives detailed information on how to draft most classic quilting designs. Gwen offers quilting retreats at her Beaver Island home on Lake Michigan, and her quilts have been shown in many exhibits throughout the United States.

Mary Stori is a lecturer, teacher, author, fashion judge, and quilter whose work has appeared and won awards in numerous national shows. In addition to her own books, *The Wholecloth Garment Stori* and *The Stori Book of Embellishment,* she's written articles or been featured in 12 quilt magazines. Mary's work is often humorous and frequently features fun embellishments and fine hand quilting. She designed The Mary Stori Collection for Kona Bay Fabrics and her own line of trapunto quilting stencils for Quilting Creations. Traveling to present lectures, workshops, and fashion shows of her wearables keeps her motivated!

Debra Wagner considers herself a traditionalist in design, if not in technique. Her main interest is in developing machine methods for traditional quiltmaking. In 1992 her quilt Rail through the Rockies was designated as a Masterpiece Quilt by the National Quilting Association. Her quilts Floral Urns and Sunburst won the Bernina Award for Machine Workmanship at the 1993 and 1995 American Quilter's Society Show and Contests. Other works have been displayed in Europe and Japan. She is the author of *Teach Yourself Machine Piecing & Quilting, Striplate Piecing,* and *All Quilt Blocks Are Not Square.*

Janet Wickell has been quilting for many years, but it became a passion in 1989 when she discovered miniature quilts. For the past several years Janet has been a freelance writer and has contributed to many books for Rodale Press, including eight titles in the Classic American Quilt Collection series. She teaches quilting and hand marbling fabric, and she also enjoys herb gardening, photography, and reproducing quilt patterns in stained glass. She is the author of *Quick Little Quilts.* Janet lives in the mountains of western North Carolina with her husband, daughter, and a growing menagerie of animal friends.

Darra Duffy Williamson is the author of *Sensational Scrap Quilts* and numerous magazine articles on the subject of quiltmaking. In 1989 she was named Quilt Teacher of the Year, and she travels extensively, teaching and lecturing at guilds and quilt events. She has served as technical writer for various Rodale publications and is currently at work on a second book for the American Quilter's Society. In addition, she is an avid and knowledgeable baseball fan and maintains a notable collection of outrageous socks.

Acknowledgments

We sincerely thank the many people and companies who have generously contributed to this book.

Quiltmakers

Karen Bolesta, Cross Stitches and Willow Switches on page 64, from the Thimbleberries pattern Fireside Cozy by Lynette Jensen

Karen Kay Buckley, Mariner's Star on page 10, Buckley Family Album Quilt on page 38, Flowers and Friends on page 104, Earthly Delights on page 116

Elsie Campbell, Great-Grandma Goebel's Bridal Quilt on pages 4, 5, and 108, Pharoah's Phans on page 32, Jewel of Serenity on page 32, Little Amish Quilt on page 32, Peach Bowl Quilt on pages 32 and 80

Judy Dales, Sow in Tears, Reap in Joy on pages 38 and 41

Stan and Mary Green, Cascade Trails on page 38, quilted by Marla Hattabaugh

Barbara Lantz, Double Irish Chain on page 41

Sue Linker, Red and Green Appliqué on page 40

Doris Morelock, My Heart Condition on page 112

Suzanne Nelson, Burnished Stars on page 14; Ruffled Feathers on page 41, from the pattern Bird Parade by Gerry Kimmel; Nancy's Challenge on page 32; Bloom Where You Are Planted on page 42, from the pattern Thru Grandmother's Window by Piece O'Cake Designs; Sophie's Orchard Star on page 68

Ellen Pahl, 5-Star Quilt on page 54; Anniversary Quilt on page 60; Jake on page 96, from Alley Cats pattern from Red Wagon Originals, Linda Brannock, designer; Sweet and Simple on page 100

Dolores Rupley, Perkiomen Valley Nine Patch on page 40

Sally Schneider, Off-Centered Log Cabin on page 35, Starry Chain on page 68, Stars Galore on pages 63 and 92, Blackford's Beauty on page 56, Ninepatch on page 58

Barbara Shiffler, Amish Homage on page 40

Eloise G. Smyrl, Autumn by the Pond on pages 2, 3, and 38; Climbing the Wall on page 6

Karen Soltys, Group Therapy on page 74

Mary Stori, Spring Green on page 48 and on the cover

Sample Makers

Most of the samples were made by Doris Morelock and Jane Townswick. Additional samples were made by Sarah Dunn, Suzanne Nelson, Ellen Pahl, and Sally Schneider.

Fabrics and Supplies

American and Efird—Thread

Coats & Clark—Thread

Dritz—Markers

Fairfield Processing Corporation—Cotton and polyester batting

FiberCo. Inc.—Cotton/wool batting

Hobbs Bonded Fibers—Cotton, polyester, and wool batting

Robert Kaufman Co., Inc.—Kona Cotton Fabrics

Stearns and Foster, Mountain Mist—Cotton and polyester batting

Terry Collingham—Quilting needles

The Stencil Company—Quilting stencils

YLI—Thread

Index

INDEX

Quilting Styles

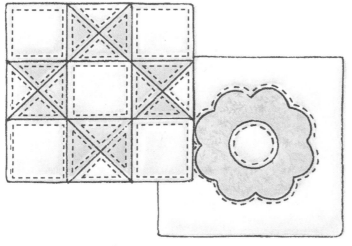

Outline Quilting

Echo Quilting

Single

Double

Crosshatch or Grid Quilting

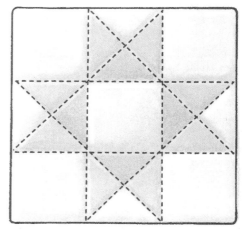

In the Ditch Quilting

Stipple Quilting

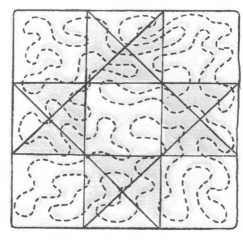

Meander Quilting